ANSWERS
for
Homeschooling

TOP **25**
QUESTIONS
CRITICS ASK

ISRAEL WAYNE

Israel Wayne has written a book that has been needed since the renewal of the homeschool movement 40 years ago. This book is the Walmart or Costco of consumer information for homeschoolers. For the new homeschooler or investigator of homeschooling, this book will give you everything you need to know, and more, in one book. The answers to the critical questions every homeschooler has at one time or another are found in this book and are easy to understand. The bottom line is that Israel's book is the first place any homeschooler should go to have their questions answered. And it could be the only place that one would have to go for this critical information about the homeschool world. Israel is owed a great deal of gratitude for finally giving us what we have needed for years. I also recommend that you look into partnering with HSLDA as they are committed to preserving and protecting our precious freedom to homeschool. Go to hslda.org for information about how you can be involved.

Mike Smith, President of HSLDA

✦ ✦ ✦ ✦

We have worked with Israel Wayne since our first event in 2012. Each year, he has been a tremendous blessing to the homeschool families that hear him speak. Now, he has distilled the wisdom and knowledge he offers in his workshops into an incredibly helpful book called *Answers for Homeschooling*. By weaving historical information and statistical data with incredibly practical advice from a homeschool veteran, Israel gives you solid answers to questions you may not even know to ask yet. Every year more and more Teach Them Diligently families discover just how wonderful Israel Wayne is, and with *Answers for Homeschooling*, he has written a "must read" for homeschool families.

David Nunnery, founder of Teach Them Diligently Homeschool Conventions, and Leslie Nunnery, author of *Teach Them Diligently: Raising Children of Promise*

✦ ✦ ✦ ✦

Do you or the people around you have some concerns about homeschooling? Israel Wayne's book answer those concerns in a thoughtful and concise manner giving you the confidence to homeschool your children. Israel is a product of the early homeschool movement and a leader in the current movement. His book, *Answers for Homeschooling* is a must read for anyone considering, or in the thick, of home educating their children.
Todd Wilson, "The Familyman," author
and conference speaker

❧ ❧ ❧ ❧

I have known Israel for many years and appreciate his desire to teach and encourage families. As I began reading this book I was impressed by the scholarship and practical nature of his insights and counsel. Even though we began teaching our four sons at home in the early 80s, and I know most of the history and key players in the home education movement, I was captivated by the information and found myself looking forward to reading more. I particularly enjoyed the pluses and minuses of each educational option. Israel has done his homework, and coupled with his experiences of being home taught himself and teaching his own children speaks with depth and practicality. This book is a wonderful resource for parents considering home education and those who are engaged in the special journey of teaching their children to love forever. I heartily commend it to you.
Steve Demme, the creator of Math-U-See, founder
of Building Faith Families, and a frequent speaker
at home education conferences

❧ ❧ ❧ ❧

Many families fail to consider homeschooling seriously because of misconceptions about what homeschooling involves. In *Answers for Homeschooling,* Israel Wayne and his wife, Brook, dispel those misconceptions by answering nearly every question about homeschooling that parents might have. There has never been a time when it has been more vital to rescue our children from the intellectual, moral, and spiritual pathologies of government schools, and I am convinced that the information provided in *Answers for Homeschooling* will lead many more families to experience the joys and rewards of homeschooling.

Bruce Shortt, author of *The Harsh Truth About Public Schools*

✦ ✦ ✦ ✦

When my friend Israel asked me to review his new book, *Answers for Homeschooling*, I raised the very question he said his readers would probably ask, "Why another book on homeschooling?" As I started to read the book, however, I found myself saying, "Yes! This book is needed!" Like Israel (even though I wasn't homeschooled), my late husband Chris Klicka — who Israel mentions in his book — and I taught all seven of our children at home in the early days of the modern homeschool movement. Chris's legal work with HSLDA in the 1980s and his books on homeschooling in the 1990s, *The Right Choice: Homeschooling* and *The Heart of Homeschooling* were instrumental in helping to create a free and supportive climate homeschooling families now freely enjoy. However, that freedom isn't guaranteed. Because of this, Israel not only makes a compelling case for why we need to learn about the roots of this truly miraculous movement of parent-led education in America, he helps parents understand how very possible it is for them to provide best what their children need. He invites you to raise the challenging questions many ask concerning home education, and then adeptly answers them. This book will help equip you, the parent, as you consider embarking on one of the most exciting and rewarding journeys with your children!

Tracy Klicka, homeschool writer and director of development for the Home School Foundation

✤ ✤ ✤ ✤

As the home education movement is growing by the millions of children in America and around the world, many parents have questions. Homeschooling pioneer Israel Wayne provides helpful and balanced answers to the most common questions posed. This book will help parents avoid common pitfalls and help them to succeed in the discipleship of their children.

Kevin Swanson, *Generations* Radio Host

First printing: February 2018

ISBN: 978-1-68344-110-6
ISBN: 978-1-61458-643-2 (digital)
Library of Congress Number: 2017962769

Please consider requesting that a copy of this volume be purchased by your local library system.

Printed in the United States of America

Please visit our website for other great titles:
www.masterbooks.com

For information regarding author interviews, please contact the publicity department at (870) 438-5288.

Master Books®
A Division of New Leaf Publishing Group
www.masterbooks.com

Contents

Special Thanks and Acknowledgments

As a special thank you, I'd like to thank my mother for homeschooling me, my wife for loving me, my children for letting me experiment on them as a parent, my sister Sony for proofreading the manuscript, Randy Pratt for suggesting the concept for the book, Tim Dudley for being the bravest Christian publisher on the planet, Laura Welch and Craig Froman for their editing expertise, and the entire Master Books team for creating a biblical worldview curriculum that isn't merely "Christian in name only." We love you guys! And finally to Jesus, without whom nothing is possible, but with whom all things are possible!

Introduction

I casually mentioned the creation of this book on social media, and in typical fashion, someone shot back with a snarky response. (That predictable Internet phenomenon probably needs to be addressed in a book somewhere!) The reply was, "Why does anyone need another book on homeschooling? Everything you could possibly say has already been said by others in books that are already published. And for that matter, a simple Google search could answer any one of these questions just as easily . . . for free!"

I'm pretty sure encouragement isn't that person's spiritual gift. Just a hunch. But it raises a valid question, "Why is this book important?"

One of the things to consider when getting information is the experience and reliability of the source. Many of you may not know me, so I'd like to take a minute to give you my experience in the homeschooling movement.

Who Is Israel Wayne?

My family was one of the very first families to begin homeschooling in the United States during what I call "the modern-day homeschooling movement." Homeschooling is as old as Adam and Eve, and 6,000 years of family life since creation. But in our day and age, it feels like a very new experiment.

My older sister was taken out of kindergarten in 1978, and we began our adventure as homeschoolers. In 1988, my mother became the founding publisher of the *Home School Digest (HSD)* magazine (it went on to become the longest-running national

Christian homeschooling periodical). Her magazine provided a launching pad for many of the homeschooling speakers and writers of the 1980s, 1990s, 2000s, and beyond.

One of the blessings of this was the many mentoring relationships I was able to form with the leaders and pioneers of the homeschooling movement. I read their books and articles, attended their seminars, and welcomed them into our home (as well as visited them in their homes).

I graduated from my homeschooling high school experience in 1991, at a time when homeschooling was not even legal in all states. In January of 1993 I began working as the marketing director for *HSD*, and wrote my first article in 1994 on the HR-6 bill (a huge national power-grab that threatened to require teacher certification for all homeschooling parents in America). The response against that bill was so massive that it shut down the telephone switchboards at the U.S. Capitol. That experience put homeschooling on the map like nothing had previously.

In 1995, I began speaking at homeschooling conferences, which I have done every year since. (I have spoken at hundreds of events over the years). In January of 1999 I married my wife, Brook, who was also home educated (since 1983). Her family was instrumental in starting the homeschooling movement in Arizona. My first book on homeschooling (*Homeschooling from a Biblical Worldview)* was published in 2000.

My family was featured in a cover story on homeschooling for *TIME Magazine* in 2001, and I've been featured on dozens of national radio and television shows discussing home education. I have been a regular columnist for three national homeschooling magazines: *HSD, Home School Enrichment,* and *The Old Schoolhouse.* I have been featured regarding homeschooling in publications like *WORLD Magazine* and HSLDA's *Court Report.*

At the date of this writing, my wife and I have nine children, ages 2 to 17. Our children have always been home educated, and, by God's grace, always will be.

To date, I have keynoted dozens of state homeschooling conferences in the United States, Japan, Russia, Mexico, and Canada. I have served on the leadership team for INCH (Michigan's official Christian state homeschooling association) and have served on an advisory council for the National Alliance of Christian Home Education Leadership. I have done marketing consulting for numerous Christian and educational publishing companies looking to market their materials to homeschoolers.

To summarize, almost nothing has ever happened in the history of the modern-day Christian homeschooling movement for which I wasn't there with a front-row seat.

So What?

Does this make me the world's greatest expert on homeschooling and parenting? Unfortunately, no. I wish it did, but in reality, I'm just like you. I'm a parent who is trying to do the best he knows, and I often fail and fall short in my attempts. I've had a lot of advantages and many great mentors, but I'm still a guy trying to find his way like everyone else. I'm not perfect and don't claim to be. My children sin like everyone else, and their dad has days where he pulls his hair out just like you do. (Okay, my hair is probably a little further gone than yours!)

What I want to assure you is that I'm not a second-year homeschooling mommy blogger. Much of the information you find online regarding homeschooling is coming from new, enthusiastic writers who have a lot of opinions but not much experience. Personally, I think that is a wonderful thing! We need more of those writers, not less! I'm so thankful they are there. But I think we also need to hear the voices of people who have been there.

I was homeschooled in a day when it was against the law, and you could be taken away from your family if you got caught. I remember before homeschooling was even a term, let alone a socially acceptable idea. In fact, my family was in court several times, defending our right to home educate. I have the battle scars from almost 40 years of being in this fight for parental control over education. I have dedicated decades of my life and have spent as many as 200 nights a year on the road (mostly with my family) ministering to and equipping other homeschooling families. I'm not shooting from the hip here. What you will get in this book is real, honest, direct, and genuine guidance and counsel. I'll share what I know, what I'm confident in, and I'll be forthright when I'm uncertain about something. I even deferred two chapters to my wife, as I'm not an expert in those areas (home and time management).

A Unique Angle

What makes this book special, besides having the dual perspective of a homeschooled student / homeschooling father, is the fact that we want to equip you to have confidence in your decision to home educate, and we want to prepare you to defend your choice to the skeptics you will inevitably face along the way.

Not everyone will rejoice over your decision to homeschool. As you read my answers to these questions, I hope the issues will be settled in your own mind, and that you can use my approach as suggestions for how to respond when people level these questions/ accusations against you. This book serves as a handy, bullet-point companion for my larger and more comprehensive treatise on a biblical philosophy of schooling: *Education: Does God Have an Opinion?*

That book is the big picture; this book is more of the nuts and bolts. That book gives a biblical apologetic for the *what* and *why* of homeschooling; this book deals more with the *how*. If you have not done so, I strongly encourage you to grab a copy of that book, as I believe it will be potentially life-changing for you.

Thank you for taking the time to read this book. I pray it will equip and strengthen you for your task. Please share it with friends!

CHAPTER 1

Is Homeschooling Legal?

For the 6,000 or so years of history, parents were primarily responsible for the teaching and training of their children. Formal schooling of any kind was usually relegated to a small percentage of students (often from the most wealthy or influential families).

Government-run schooling is, for the most part, a very new conception in world history. The Prussians began promoting government-controlled, compulsory education in the late 18th century. In the United States, a Unitarian named Horace Mann began promoting compulsory attendance laws in Massachusetts in 1840. The first laws were passed there in 1852. In 1918, Mississippi became the final state to adopt some form of compulsory attendance requirements.

Once these laws mandating attendance in government schools were in place, it criminalized truancy and absenteeism. The government now had a complete monopolistic lock-down on schooling in America. It was not until 1925, in a landmark Supreme Court case entitled *Pierce vs. The Society of Sisters*, that the Roman Catholic Church in America gained exemption from compulsory attendance laws and earned the legal freedom to start their own, competing parochial schools.

An Amish man named Jonas Yoder eventually won the *Wisconsin vs. Yoder* case in 1972, allowing the Amish communities to do the same. Yoder had a religious conviction against sending his children to schools where they would be taught values that conflicted with his religious faith. This case opened the door for other Protestant churches to freely establish privately-funded Christian schools that offered explicitly religious instruction for students.

Homeschooling Begins Again

Between 1979 and 1983, Dr. James Dobson had Dr. Raymond Moore on his radio show a few times to discuss his research on early childhood development. Dr. Moore was an advocate (based on his studies) for delaying formal schooling for young children, especially boys who were struggling with reading. On the broadcast, he encouraged parents to keep their children at home and let them develop until they were older before sending them to a formal school. He quickly began advocating for home education as a general principle, as he saw the success parents were having in teaching their own children at home.

Because of these broadcasts, thousands of families around the nation began taking their children out of public school (or never sending them in the first place). This was met with legal opposition from local school boards and truancy officers. These families were violating their state compulsory attendance laws by refusing to send their child to a government or private school.

In 1983, Michael Farris and J. Michael Smith founded the Home School Legal Defense Association (HSLDA) and were soon joined by a young lawyer named Christopher J. Klicka (formerly of the Rutherford Association). They began to represent families who had decided to home educate but were facing truancy charges from school districts.

That same year, Christian state organizations began to form, and state-wide homeschooling conventions were established. Parents could come and hear speakers teach on home education, and they could buy curriculum from vendors in the convention hall.

The Legal Battle

Christian school administrators, many of whom had faced their own legal battles in a fight for exclusively Christian education, began to take notice of these families. Many of them allowed homeschoolers to enroll in their school, as private school students, but to continue to do the bulk of their teaching at home. The private schools kept all the records and did standardized testing (in many cases) to appease authorities. Because private schools were not mandated by law to hand over the private records of these students, it was almost impossible for these families to be prosecuted, even though the students were not attending a formal school classroom.

HSLDA began working in conjunction with many state homeschooling associations to create legislation that would exempt private home educators from compulsory attendance laws. This created a new category, legally, of "homeschoolers," rather than the two previous options of "public school" and "private school." State organizations have provided important legislative work by watching their legislature each year for bills that could adversely impact homeschooling freedoms.

The Early Days

When my family began homeschooling in 1978, homeschooling as a concept was virtually unheard of. Parents who chose to keep their children at home usually did so clandestinely. Not only was homeschooling illegal, but there was also almost no support. Curriculum companies that sold to Christian schools would not sell to parents. Pastors told parishioners who chose to home educate that they were being disobedient to Scripture. They said that Romans 13 commands parents to obey all civil laws, and so they were disobeying God by trying to give their children a Christian education at home.

Because of the threat of truancy officers or child protective service workers showing up unexpectedly on your doorstep, families like ours stayed inside during school hours. We kept the curtains closed. We tried not to talk about school with our nosy neighbors (who wondered why the bus never stopped at our house). We didn't tell many people what we were doing. Grandparents and extended relatives thought we were being deprived, and believed the experiment would go totally wrong. They were convinced we would grow up to be social misfits, be unemployed, and have no idea how to relate to others in the "real world."

The stakes were high because if you were caught homeschooling, your children could be taken away from you. Your parental rights could be terminated and your children could be placed into foster care (where government schooling was mandated). It was a scary time. Many homeschooled children actually had escape routes planned of how they would hide if social workers came to get them.

It's hard to believe that we aren't talking about some communist nation during the Cold War, but the "land of the free and the home of the brave" during the 1970s and '80s. My own family was in court on several occasions to defend our right to home educate. I remember the fear I had that I would not be able to continue living with my family and would not be allowed to homeschool. On two different occasions, because of run-ins with the courts (my second and sixth grade years), my older sister and I were placed in private Christian schools for a year until the smoke cleared, and then my mother promptly went back to home educating us (after everyone had forgotten about the ordeal).

It is a blessing that such scenes are almost a distant memory in today's homeschooling climate. It is important for newer homeschoolers to learn the history of the modern-day home education movement. I have created a website and interviewed many of the pioneers, allowing them to share their experiences and stories. It is called HomeschoolPioneers.com.

The long and arduous battle for legal freedoms for all homeschoolers is told in a unique book by the late Christopher Klicka, entitled, *Home School Heroes: The Struggle & Triumph of Home Schooling in America.*

Homeschooling Is Legal!

Today, homeschooling is legal in all 50 states and many countries around the world. Almost everyone knows someone who is being, or was, home educated. Homeschooling is almost mainstream, with people from all walks of life choosing to take control of their own child's education.

Legal requirements vary quite a bit from place to place, with little to extensive regulations. Some states require annual reporting to a local school board. Others require some form of standardized testing. Still others require a certain number of hours for formal instruction, usually on specifically outlined academic subjects. Since there are no federal laws regulating homeschooling (and most homeschoolers want to keep the federal government completely out of the education business altogether), there is much variation on a state level.

The best way to stay informed regarding the laws in your state is to become a member of HSLDA and your Christian state homeschooling association (which you can locate from HSLDA's website).

The Future of Homeschooling

The biggest threat to homeschooling in the future, in my view, is not a big federal power-grab where the government seeks to make all homeschooling illegal. Instead, I believe the greater risk is that homeschooling parents will simply give away their autonomy, and the legal freedoms that were so painfully fought and won, in exchange for "free" government handouts in the form of education vouchers for homeschoolers and other government-funded educational opportunities. Whoever pays for the education controls it.

The next generation of homeschoolers will need to learn, and know, the history of the pioneers, and not allow their work to go to waste. I will discuss this more thoroughly in the chapters on dealing with public school at home and vouchers. Homeschooling freedoms will be maintained through eternal vigilance on the part of parents and organizations who are committed to the principles of liberty and parent-directed and -controlled education. We have gained so much freedom. Now it is up to you and your children to maintain and preserve those freedoms.

CHAPTER 2

Are You Qualified to Teach Your Child?

My own homeschooling experience was rather unique. My mother had a bad experience in government schools when she was growing up. She was dyslexic and was made to feel stupid because she wasn't good at academics, so she quit trying to work within that system and essentially dropped out in ninth grade.

It was probably this background that made her more willing to take my older sister, Sony, out of school when she had a bad experience in kindergarten. Homeschooling was not only *uncool* in 1978, but it was also *illegal*. We ended up being in court several times over the years fighting charges of truancy because of the compulsory attendance laws that were on the books in almost every state.

By the time I entered high school, my mother was a single parent with two teenagers and four little girls to raise. In case you missed the math in the scenario, I was the only boy in a family with five sisters! (Feel free to extend lots of sympathy here!)

What If I Never Learned a Certain Subject Myself?

I was also dyslexic and struggled academically. I desired to finish up my studies as quickly as possible so that I could get a job. My mother told me that I could do something that would today be called "Accelerated Distance Learning" for high school. She explained that if I doubled up my studies, I could complete four years of high school in two. She provided the curriculum and classroom video instruction at home so that I had a "personal tutor" to guide me through the material, using Abeka Academy, which was a very time-intensive, and fairly rigorous, academic approach. I didn't have much of a social life for two years! But I finished 12th grade a week or so before my 16th birthday, and immediately got a job working 40 hours a week.

My mother simply didn't have time to hold my hand all the way through my studies. Neither did she feel obligated to cram my head full of every fact and detail that could possibly be learned in the universe. But she had supplied me with the basics, and taught me how to learn. By engaging me in meaningful discussions throughout my high school years, and grading my tests, she provided accountability to ensure that I was completing the assigned work.

What Are the Essentials of Teaching?

My mother informed me that her responsibility to me was to:

1. Teach me how to read
2. Teach me how to think/reason
3. Teach me how to study/learn

She said, "If you know how to read, how to reason, and how to find the information you need, then you can teach yourself anything you need to know in life." Her goal was not so much to teach me, as it was to teach me how to successfully teach myself.

She used to tell me, "In the real world, you don't see people walking down the street carrying a stack of textbooks under their arm. That's not how adults learn."

My experience in high school mirrored what research from Dr. Brian Ray discovered when examining the standardized achievement tests of homeschooled students:

A parent's education background has no substantive effect on their children's home school academic performance.
Home educated students' test scores remain between the

80th and 90th percentiles, whether their mothers have a college degree or did not complete high school.[1]

According to Dr. Ray's research, a child in the government school whose parent has a master's degree or a teaching certificate will score 25 to 30 percent lower, on average, than a homeschooled student whose parent has only a high school diploma or less. In homeschooling, it is the customized context and the parental involvement that make the difference, not the academic pedigree of the parents.

What Makes a Good Teacher?

What makes a good teacher is not IQ. It is not being an expert at knowing random facts and information. It is caring about the student and understanding their strengths and weaknesses. It is helping to walk alongside them, encouraging and equipping them to overcome hurdles and difficulties. A good teacher is a good listener. A good teacher is a good example, modeling good character, work, and study habits.

I remember years ago talking to a friend of mine who was a government school teacher. She told me that her goal was to stay one week ahead of her students. She said that she didn't remember most of the material she was teaching (because she didn't use it in everyday life), but as long as she stayed just a few steps ahead of her students, everything worked out okay.

The wonderful thing about homeschooling is that you, as a parent, have the opportunity to learn alongside your student. It's a great way for you to review, or fill in the gaps of your own education. Don't be embarrassed if you don't know everything. No one does. Even professional school teachers don't know everything there is to know about the subject in which they specialize. They frequently must look up answers or ask others for advice or direction.

The fact is that no one knows your child, or cares about him, more than you do. God gave your child to you, not to the government or the church or to another family. He gave that child to you, because He believes that you are the best-equipped person in the world to raise him or her.

What about Gaps in Their Education?

Most students are strong in certain subjects and weak in others. We obviously want our children to be as well-rounded as possible, but we must recognize certain innate limits. Most people choose the career they do because it best fits their inclinations and aptitudes.

If your child has good study and research habits, he or she can learn whatever may be lacking in their education. In high school, my mother insisted that I do Algebra 1 and Chemistry, even though she knew that I probably wouldn't ever use those subjects in my future life and career. She wanted me to develop the discipline of studying subjects that I didn't necessarily enjoy. But she did not insist that I study trigonometry or calculus. She said that I would simply be wasting my time, considering my interests lay elsewhere. I really haven't used any of those subjects, but I can see the importance of using wisdom and balance in determining which subjects to emphasize and which to overlook. We only have so much time in life, and we need to learn to say no to some subjects so that we can say yes to the ones that are the most important.

How Can I Learn How to Teach?

Utilizing a curriculum that contains a good lesson plan scheduling system, or buying one if you are creating your own mix-and-match curriculum, is very helpful. One of the most important things is to ensure that you don't destroy your child's love of learning. There is far more to learning than studying textbooks.

Create short-term and long-term educational goals. Develop a strategy, including required resources, and a timeline for how to accomplish your goals. Encourage your students to do independent study and research, including reading books or doing field trips that may help them to understand the lessons they are learning. Make sure you reward your students' successes and be careful that you don't demoralize them when they fall short of their or your goals. Remember to verbally encourage and affirm them as they grow and develop. Keep an open dialogue going so they know that they can ask questions without being emotionally shot down or discouraged. Surround yourself with local and/or online support networks of other homeschooling parents who can help you with their knowledge and experience. Increasingly, there are online social media groups of parents who use a particular curriculum so you can gain advice and counsel from other parents who use the same materials you do. Sometimes, the authors of the curriculum will join the discussions and answer questions directly. I also highly recommend attending homeschooling conferences and attending teaching workshops conducted by various experts in their field. It is invaluable information that can save you so much hassle and even years of regret by getting things off on the right foot from the beginning. You can find a list of state homeschooling associations, along with their websites and their annual conferences, by visiting www.HSLDA.org.

Endnotes:
1. Dr. Brian D. Ray, National Home Education Research Institute, 1997 study, https://www.hslda.org/docs/study/ray1997/07.asp.

CHAPTER 3

How Can You Afford to Homeschool?

A Christian ministry did an email survey to their readership of several hundred thousand evangelical Christians. The survey targeted Christian parents, asking if they would choose Christian education for their children if cost was not an issue. In other words, if someone else would pay for your child's education, would you choose homeschooling or Christian schooling over government schooling? While the report was never published, I was told privately by a friend of mine at the organization who conducted that survey that 77 percent said they would prefer homeschooling or Christian education if it were provided for free.

This tells me that money is the number one reason that most Christian parents choose government schooling for their children. Since about 80 to 85 percent of Evangelical parents send their children to secular schools, it clearly is not because they think it's the best option. It is because they feel they can't afford it (or don't want to make it a financial priority).

Yet other families do see the need for a Christian education and truly desire it for their children. They just haven't figured out how to get things squared away to be able to support their family on one income and/or how to afford to buy the needed curriculum.

How Much Does It Cost to Homeschool?

The truth is, home education is a bargain compared to the amount of money that is spent on each child in the government school setting. It costs 20 times the amount, on average, for a child to be "schooled" in a brick-and-mortar, government-run school than it does for parents to teach that same child at home. According to the National Center for Education Statistics:

> Total expenditures for public elementary and secondary schools in the United States in 2013–14 amounted to $634 billion, or $12,509 per public school student enrolled in the fall (in constant 2015–16 dollars). Total expenditures included $11,222 per student in current expenditures, which includes salaries, employee benefits, purchased services, and supplies. Total expenditures also included $939 per student in capital outlay (expenditures for property and for buildings and alterations completed by school district staff or contractors) and $348 for interest on school debt.[1]

Dr. Brian Ray of the National Home Education Research Institute says:

> Families engaged in home-based education are not dependent on public, tax-funded resources for their children's education. The finances associated with their homeschooling likely represent over $27 billion that American taxpayers do not have to spend, annually, since these children are not in public schools. . . . Taxpayers spend nothing on most homeschool students, and homeschool families spend an average of $600 per student (annually) for their education.[2]

How Much Does Curriculum Cost?

There are several approaches to curriculum. For instance, you can buy an entire "grade in a box" from a traditional textbook publisher and usually spend less than $400 for the kit. The higher grades will, of course, cost more than the lower ones. If you go with a video curriculum, or an online program with video instruction, that can be $1,000 or more per child, per year.

You can, however, utilize many methods to cut down on your curriculum expenses. One way is to buy new when the publisher runs sales. Most publishers have a couple of times a year when they reduce the price of their materials. Others will offer special conference rates at your state's annual homeschooling convention. Some publishers will offer a special "scratch 'n dent" sale, where you can buy unused display copies of their textbooks that may have been scuffed, or corners bent, during shipping to and from conferences.

There are also used curriculum fairs, online curriculum swaps, and even Facebook groups where people sell their used (or new pre-owned curriculum) at a discounted price. Often a family will buy an expensive program, only to realize that it isn't working as they had hoped. They will resell it for pennies on the dollar, just to recoup some of their cost, and pass it on to someone who can use it.

There are also library sales and used book sales, many of which offer wonderful finds for frugal homeschoolers. Old historical books in public libraries are being thrown away in exchange for newer novels and popular books for children and teens. The older books often contain stories about Lewis and Clark, Daniel Boone, Kit Carson, Betsy Ross, or other great American heroes. The newer books (often recommended reading in local government schools) are often about teen dating relationships, vampires, witchcraft, and much more. It's sad to see how people's values are shifting, but our family has really benefitted from the rejection of these older books. The library's loss is our family's gain!

Homeschooling for Free!

When my family began homeschooling in 1978, it was against the law to teach your own children at home. For the most part, no one had ever heard of such a radical concept. In those early days, Christian curriculum providers had created materials for Christian schools, but they would not sell directly to parents. So, families like my own set out to create our own curriculum.

While not necessarily preferable as a long-term solution, there are ways to home educate entirely for free. If you have access to a local library, you can create your own unit studies using books that you check out at no cost. You can supplement with free educational videos online. You can take your children to historical locations (many of which are free) that may be right in your area.

There are also many homeschooling parents who would be willing to loan curriculum to you that they are not currently using. We have done this with other families whom we sensed needed this.

If you truly want to homeschool your children, I believe you can eventually find a way. My mother homeschooled six children on absolutely nothing (for a season). The main issue is one of the heart. Are you totally committed to the concept of giving your children an exclusively Christian education? If so, God will show Himself strong on your behalf.

An extensive list of free homeschooling resources can be found at www.hslda.org/highschool/FreeResources.asp.

Help and Support

While not an option for every family, The Home School Foundation,[3] which is a non-profit division of HSLDA (Home School Legal Defense Association), gives grants for qualifying families in certain situations (widows, for example) to help purchase homeschooling curriculum.

Several state homeschooling associations (Texas, Louisiana, and Alabama come to mind) have raised support to help families who lost their school books due to flooding because of hurricanes. Some curriculum publishers have offered to donate free (or replace) curriculum to families in such situations. On occasion (although it is not as frequent as I'd like to see), even local churches have come alongside families to help them create a financial and logistical roadmap to be able to home educate their children.

One way our family saves money is by buying textbooks that are reusable for younger students. We may pay a bit more up front for these resources, but it enables us to be able to pass them down to other children. Our overall cost for homeschooling nine children is quite low, because we do not have the same investment with each child (just additional student workbooks).

Financial Freedom

Oftentimes, the inability to afford to homeschool comes from a financial lifestyle that isn't conducive to living on a single income. Sometimes, the circumstances are beyond one's control (massive hospital bills, ongoing special needs care, loss of a home, etc.). In most cases, however, it is either that a family has expectations of living "the American dream," and they won't make the sacrifices necessary to ensure that they can live on one income (perhaps having one vehicle, foregoing cable television, or doing without eating out or going on expensive vacations).

In many other cases, a family has buried themselves into deep debt because of poor financial management. It is my advice that families who find themselves in such situations seek out budget counseling through their local churches or through a qualified financial consultant. They need to create a game plan to reduce their debt and create a scenario where at least one parent can be a full-time stay-at-home parent, or they can toggle their work schedules so someone is home to teach the children.

You may not always be able to go from where you are now to where you want to be in one easy step, but having a workable game plan is essential. As I discuss in the chapter, "Won't I Be Wasting My Own Education?" having two full-time incomes is often not as financially advantageous as we have been led to believe.

Having a financial plan, and accountability from your church elders or budget coach, can help you to break free from debt and poor financial management. I hear parents, who make more money than my wife and I do, say that they cannot afford to homeschool their three children. My wife and I successfully homeschool our large family on less money than they make. There are many families who make it work. Perhaps you need to consult with some large homeschooling families who have learned how to homeschool successfully on very little income.

Should Poor Children Be Punished for Being Poor?

People often tell me, "Some people just cannot afford to homeschool," the implication being that they need to send their child to an anti-Christian school if they are below a certain financial threshold. I just don't understand that logic. Why punish the poor child with anti-Christian indoctrination simply because his parents don't make very much money? Is that what Jesus wants? Does He think to Himself, "I want all of My children to be educated in the fear of the Lord . . . except for the poor ones. I want them to learn that they evolved from pond scum and that they don't have a defined gender."

I don't think so. From my perspective, I can't afford NOT to homeschool! What does it profit me if I gain the whole world (financially) and risk my child's soul?

In my book *Full-Time Parenting: A Guide to Family-Based Discipleship*, I have chapters on "Living on a Single Income" and "Considerations Before You Start Your Own Business." I'd direct people to these chapters for more information on how to make things work logistically for your family.

Suppose we lived in a hypothetical universe where there were only two choices:

1. Send my child to an anti-Christian school where they would be lied to and given an anti-Christian world-view for seven hours a day

2. Have my child sit and stare at a wall for seven hours every day

I would always choose the latter because at least then I'm not having to deal with a deficit. If I had to make up time in the evening with only two to three hours of parental involvement a day, I'd rather have a scenario where I wasn't having to decon-struct and deprogram my children each night from the falsehoods they had been taught at school during the day.

Thankfully, none of us are truly faced with this false dichotomy. There are many ways that children learn, and almost none of them require a classroom. Never confuse schooling and education. They are NOT synonymous terms. Children with a low income can learn the truth very easily, and be prepared for life quite adequately, without ever stepping foot into a formal school classroom. We just need to have our minds renewed so we learn to think differently about what education actually is and how we can best facilitate it.

Endnotes

1. https://nces.ed.gov/fastfacts/display.asp?id=66.
2. Dr. Brian D. Ray, National Home Education Research Institute, March 23, 2016, https://nheri.org/research/research-facts-on-homeschooling.html.
3. https://homeschoolfoundation.org.

CHAPTER 4

Is That How It's Done in Public School?

While the government school classroom model is increasingly becoming a one-size-fits-all, standardized approach, homeschooling is exactly the opposite. Homeschooling represents decentralization and individualization.

Which educational philosophy is best for you and your child? I would suggest that each child may respond completely differently, as each child is uniquely created and designed by God. No two children are the same. But while there are learning styles to be considered, there are also teaching styles. Let's examine some of the most popular methods or educational approaches for homeschoolers.

Traditional Textbook Approach

If you attended a traditional classroom school (and most parents have), this is the style with which you are most familiar. In school, you use traditional textbooks and/or workbooks, complete with teacher guides and answer keys. There are many publishers who sell these materials to homeschoolers. Many of these programs, however, did not begin as homeschooling products. In some cases, these were designed with the Christian school classroom in mind, and were, at best, repackaged for a homeschooling audience.

The Upside

The good thing about these publishers is that they spent a lot of money to develop their materials, since they had the backing of the Christian school movement, and therefore the materials are comprehensive, complete, and usually respectable in their overall presentation.

You can buy a package of "second grade" or "eighth grade," and all the major subjects will be represented. You don't have to mix and match with different books from different publishers. It's all together in one comprehensive set. Some of the most popular publishers of the past couple of decades have been Abeka, Bob Jones, ACE (School of Tomorrow), Alpha Omega, Christian Light Education, and Rod & Staff Publishers.

Our family primarily uses curriculum from Master Books, an excellent Christian publisher who integrates a biblical worldview into every subject and grade level. We love the fact that we don't have to neglect professional quality printing and design (their materials are equal or better to any secular publisher) or academic excellence. Many of their textbooks are written by PhDs and other experts in various fields. People sometimes ask if their child will receive an inferior academic curriculum if they choose homeschooling. The answer is no. You can get anything a student in the government schools can get, but far more that is exclusively published for home educators.

The Downside

Cost can be a downside to this approach. Everything is laid out for you, and it's convenient, but often you pay extra for convenience. This approach can be relatively expensive (as much as $1,500 per year, per student).

Because these products were often created with the classroom in mind, many parents find these materials difficult to use in the home with a single student. The teacher's guides are sometimes designed for teaching multiple students all the same grade (something you don't find frequently in families), and there is very little ability to adapt the materials to a specific student's needs.

Online Schooling

For many years, there have been computer software programs that guide a student through his or her coursework. These programs still exist, but today there are also Internet-only options that involve online tests and often online video tutorials.

There are two variations of this: government schooling at home (virtual public or charter schools) and private, online academies.

There are private online programs that are completely free (an assortment of compiled courses that individuals or businesses have put together). There are also very expensive programs. One of the most popular costs about $1,500 per student, per year, for high school studies. As technology becomes increasingly dominant in our society, this option will likely be increasingly popular.

The Upside

Online programs require little to no parental involvement. Students can be guided by a pre-selected course or have accountability through an online teacher or program that checks their progress and grades their work. This scenario may be the best option if, for instance, a single-parent needs to work a job, but the student has a grandparent at home who can make sure the student stays on task.

The Downside

Online programs require little to no parental involvement. In my view, homeschooling is all about family discipleship, so the idea that a child will sit passively and bond with the Internet all day isn't ideal in my view. I have heard of some parents choosing a free program (that often uses public online videos or articles) and putting their child online to do their studies all day while the two of them go to work — sometimes leaving the child completely alone to do "homeschooling" online.

There are so many ways that is a horrible idea. First, it's probably against the law in your state. Second, how do you know what they are actually doing all day on the Internet? Unless there is an incredible system to track all Internet activity, this is setting yourself up for failure in terms of your child's moral purity. Children who are unsupervised often begin gaming, visiting porn sites, chatting with strangers on social media, and much more. Internet filters can only go so far in keeping the child restricted. There is never a replacement for parental involvement.

With online programs, you typically get what you pay for. The free programs tend to lack comprehensive instruction, and it is likely that your child will receive a sub-par academic education. And the expensive programs are, well, just that . . . expensive.

Unit Studies

A unit study is a unique approach where the focus of learning is all about studying one topic at a time. Imagine, for example, that you wanted to study the American Revolutionary War. You would center the entire focus on that period, and would seek to integrate every subject into that unit. For English and grammar, you could have your children read the founding documents of our nation, and write their own essays. History is obviously innate to the topic. Science could deal with Franklin's early experiments with electricity or his other many inventions. Geography would be incorporated as you discuss the battles and movement of the armies. Civics and government are clearly embedded into the fabric of this study.

The Upside

For parents who love to be creative, this is clearly a great approach. In a way, you are creating your own curriculum, using materials from films to library books or field trips to history sites. This is also probably the easiest way to teach multiple grades at once. Every student will learn a little differently as you journey through this topic together. It's a great way to incorporate fun and a lot of family unity into your studies.

The Downside

Not everyone has the inclination, or time, to be creative. Creating your own curriculum is not appealing to someone who really wants everything laid out for them in advance. It is also difficult if you are keeping records for high school transcripts. How do you decide how many credits to give for your work? It's easier when it's already outlined for you by a curriculum developer.

Classical Model

Based on the Greco-Roman tradition, the Classical model incorporates what has been called The Trivium and Quadrivium. The Trivium consists of three distinct learning segments: Latin (grammar), logic, and rhetoric. The Quadrivium consists of arithmetic, geometry, music, and astronomy. During the Renaissance in Europe, these approaches to learning received a new resurgence. The homeschooling movement has latched on to the Classical Approach in a huge way. There are both secular and Christian versions of classical education.

The Upside

The Classical Approach is usually very academically rigorous. It encourages critical thinking and developing clear defense of one's beliefs. There are formal groups of homeschoolers who sometimes meet in what is called a "Practicum," to support each other and help others along. It's essentially a homeschooling co-op with a Classical focus. The Classical Approach helps people to understand the roots of Western culture, through the writings of the Greek philosophers, poets, and story tellers.

The Downside

Some groups approach the Classical Approach from a distinctively biblical worldview, but others do not. The ancient Greeks and Romans were not Christians. They had a neo-pagan worldview, that is, in many ways antithetical to the teachings of the Bible. There are some programs, even Christian ones, which tend to glorify the Greek model, and encourage even young children to dive into Greek mythology. They promote Greek philosophers like Plato, and promote his ideas. There is no doubt these thinkers influenced the people who shaped our current culture (including America's founding fathers), but there should be more critical analysis of these authors than mere promotion of their ideas. If a classical program is not diligent in pointing out the wrong beliefs of these authors, Christian children may be inclined to be shaped, negatively, by their perspective.

Unschooling

In the late 1970s, a non-Christian named John Holt began promoting a concept that he called "Unschooling." The idea is that when you come out of government education, you need to take a completely different look at things. You need to be "unschooled." His view was that institutional government schooling was unnatural for children, and that life made a better school than a formal, structured classroom. Unschooling tends to eschew traditional textbooks and formal learning environments for the elements of nature, outdoor education, hands-on learning, and practical, everyday experiences. Students usually pursue their own interests rather than follow any prescribed coursework. One Christian author has a similar approach that she has called "Relaxed Homeschooling." Others refer to it as "self-directed learning."

The Upside

Government schooling should never be the model for how we think about education. Education is not schooling, and schooling is not education. We should never confuse the two. Students who are unschooled are frequently exceptional at whatever topic has driven their interest.

The Downside

The view of unschooling set out by John Holt, and held by his most ardent followers, rejects the notion of original sin and denies the biblical teaching that children are inclined to sin if left to themselves. The biblical view, outlined in Proverbs 22:6, insists that children do not know which way they should go. They need parents, who are older and wiser, to discern their course for them. Catering to a child's whims and wishes often leads to them having some strengths, especially being advanced in their personal interests, but it also can leave them quite deficient in any area they are not naturally inclined to study of their own volition.

Delight-Directed Learning

In some ways, this approach can mirror unschooling. This can mean either no textbooks at all in teaching your children, or you can incorporate them, but only to the extent that it matches the interest of the student. The main objective is to keep the child from losing interest in learning by allowing them to pursue their inclinations. Christians who believe in guiding their children (not merely letting them find their way as many radical unschoolers would) would say they are being involved parents. This approach has also been called "Lifeschooling." These parents are merely helping the child tap into their own unique talents and proclivities. The pros and cons of this would be very similar to unschooling.

Principle Approach®

Two Christian educators named Verna Hall and Rosalie Slater developed a philosophy of education they called the Principle Approach®. It is based on the Hebraic method of the teacher as a mentor. It has a strong emphasis on the founding of the American form of government and is very focused on the providential aspects of early American history.

There are seven foundational principles of the Principle Approach®:

1. God's Principle of Individuality
2. The Principle of Christian Self-Government
3. The Principle of Christian Character
4. Conscience as the Most Sacred Property
5. The Christian Form of Our Government

6. Planting the Seed of Local Self-Government
7. American Political Union

The concept of self-government is that a person is governed by God's law, from within his or her own heart and will. When a society demonstrates self-government, it needs little external force. When a society rejects a moral law and self-government under that law, it devolves into chaos and anarchy, and requires external force to keep it in check.

The Upside

Students trained in this approach have some of the highest biblical worldview test scores of any teaching method. This approach points students back to God as the source of all moral law and ethics. Its study of the founding fathers and founding documents of America definitely helps students to become grounded in history, free-market economics, law, government, and civics.

The Downside

In my view, it is easy in this approach to focus exclusively on the positive aspects of early American history, and overlook or gloss over some of the not-so-good stains on our history, even shortcomings and failures of the founding fathers themselves. History must be brutally honest and always tell the truth. That includes telling the whole truth. The government schools do not tell the truth about history, in that they have reinvented it to remove Christianity's positive influence, and retold the story through their postmodern lenses. We should not make the mistake of doing the same — of telling only half of the story. I personally feel that much of the Principle Approach® material is exclusively positive of America's foundations and, therefore, errs in terms of balance.

Charlotte Mason Approach

Charlotte Mason (1842–1923) was a British educator who wrote a series of six books outlining her philosophy of education. Her books were repopularized in the 1980s by the daughter of the late Dr. Francis Schaeffer (Susan Schaeffer MacAuley) in her book, *For the Children's Sake.* Charlotte Mason's five-book set was republished by Dean and Karen Andreola through Tyndale House Publishers.

Mason's approach emphasized reading "living books," a term she used to refer to reading real books of literature, history, or biography rather than prepackaged textbooks. Students would be expected to give verbal summaries of the books they had read. Mason recommended learning from nature and outdoor adventures and other life experiences as well.

The Upside

The Charlotte Mason method works well for a student who likes to do, rather than merely sit. It invigorates the imagination and incorporates the fine arts more comprehensively than most other approaches. It is more of a "right brain" (creative) learning approach than "left brain" (rational/logical). The artistic, creative student, especially the one who loves literature, will probably thrive under this approach. One of the greatest strengths in the Charlotte Mason approach is the guidance students receive in "narrating" back what they have learned, thereby solidifying their comprehension and increasing oral communication skills.

The Downside

While Charlotte Mason promoted a Christian education with manners and character-building for students, she did not have a biblical worldview when it came to the nature of the child. She denied the biblical doctrine of original sin (that all humans since Adam and Eve are born with a tendency toward sin and disobedience to God, rather than holiness and godliness, and are therefore sinners by both action and intent, and are guilty before God). She believed that children were born neutral — a kind of *tabula rasa* (or clean slate) as John Locke declared. There is a lot of good in her teaching, but Christians need to read discerningly.

Eclectic Approach

Finally, the dumping place for those homeschoolers who don't fit into someone else's prefabricated box . . . we have a box just for you! The Eclectic Approach is a hybrid of the best of whatever you have found to work for you and your child. Perhaps you do a little bit of Classical, and some Charlotte Mason, and some textbooks, and online, and hands-on, outdoor adventures, and field-tripping, and scrapbooking/lapbooking and make up your own curriculum as you go.

I find that a lot of homeschoolers like the curriculum-in-a-box for the first few years of homeschooling, because everything is laid out for them, and all they have to do is follow the instructions. As time goes by, many homeschoolers begin to stretch their wings and try new approaches. They often land on a hybrid method that works for their unique family.

Conclusion

The wonderful thing about homeschooling is that there can be as many different approaches as there are families and students. You can customize an approach that fits your unique teaching and learning styles. You don't have to homeschool like anyone else. You need to do what is best for your family. There is no lack of quality resources available. There are books available that discuss each of the approaches I've outlined above, so if one of them sounds like it might be a good option, do an Internet search and dive into a book that details these approaches in more depth.

CHAPTER 5

What about Accountability?

One of the biggest concerns that homeschoolers have is that they aren't doing enough academically. They fear that their student will end up being intellectually inferior to students in traditional schools, and, therefore, will be disadvantaged when it comes to his or her future life and vocation.

In short, I have two different answers to this question. There is a myriad of ways to know if your child is a "standardized" child. There are lots of standardized tests to ensure that your child is standard.

My next answer is really a question: Why would you want to?

Grades

Most parents, when they first start homeschooling, are desperately trying to recreate the government school in their home. This is not desirable. Institutional schools are predicated on the notion of mass indoctrination of masses of students.

John Taylor Gatto was an American school teacher of 29 years, author, New York State Teacher of the Year in 1991, and an eventual critic of the government school model. As part of his "recipe for empty children," he says this:

- Remove children from the business of the world until time has passed for them to learn how to self-teach.
- Age-grade them so that past and future both are muted and become irrelevant.

- Remove religion out of their lives except the hidden civil religion of appetite, and positive/negative reinforcement schedules.
- Grade, evaluate, and assess children constantly and publicly. Begin early. Make sure everyone knows his or her rank.
- Honor the highly graded. Keep grading and real-world accomplishment as strictly separated as possible so that a false meritocracy, dependent on the support of authority to continue, is created. Push the most independent kids to the margin, do not tolerate real argument.[1]

He also rather bluntly stated, "Who besides a degraded rabble would voluntarily present itself to be graded and classified like meat? No wonder school is compulsory."[2]

There have been many times when my children have been asked, "What grade are you in?" only to look at me with a blank stare, as if to say, "I have no idea what that means."

Who invented "grades" anyway? Prussian educators in the 19th century began to systematize schooling so that children were packed together by approximate age and were forced to learn the same material at the same time. This completely works against individuality and creativity.

At the time of this printing, I have nine children. None of them are standardized children. They are all completely different, with different learning styles, personalities, and interests.

At one point, I had a 15-year-old daughter doing "9th-grade" math, while my 7-year-old son was doing "6th-grade" math. This could never happen in a government school. The older daughter would probably be labeled as "learning challenged," or something of that sort (which is not true, she just isn't a math person). And my younger son would probably be labeled as "gifted" or "advanced." The fact is, very few children progress and learn at the same rate, in every subject, in every grade. We're all uniquely created with different aptitudes.

To me, it's not a matter of better or worse. It's not a race to the top. It's about each student doing the best that he or she possibly can, and learning what they need to know in order to prepare them for the life of service to which God will call them. To that end, caring, involved parents will typically be aware of the strengths and weaknesses of their home-educated child. This parent often knows exactly what topics and skills need to be covered next and has a knowledge of how the student needs to develop. Likewise, homeschooling parents are generally clued in to where each of their children stand regarding the mastery of subjects previously learned.

Comparison

In my view, it is very dangerous to compare a child to another child. Why should another child, or an average composite of a group of children, be the standard? The Apostle Paul said:

> Not that we dare to classify or compare ourselves with some of those who are commending themselves. But when they measure themselves by one another and compare them-selves with one another, they are without understanding (2 Cor. 10:12).

Paul celebrated the fact that we are not all assembly-line replicas. We are each special, unique, and distinct in our design.

> But as it is, God arranged the members in the body, each one of them, as he chose. If all were a single member, where would the body be? As it is, there are many parts, yet one body. The eye cannot say to the hand, "I have no need of you," nor again the head to the feet, "I have no need of you." On the contrary, the parts of the body that seem to be weaker are indispensable (1 Cor. 12:18–22).

What about Testing?

Two popular options for testing students are the Iowa Tests of Basic Skills (ITBS) and the California Achievement Test (CAT).

SetonTesting.com is one of the most established sites for academic assessments for homeschooled students.

Paul doesn't seem to be against the concept of testing, but the testing he recommends is quite different than that advocated by government schools.

> Examine yourselves, to see whether you are in the faith. Test yourselves. Or do you not realize this about yourselves, that Jesus Christ is in you? — unless indeed you fail to meet the test! (2 Cor. 13:5).

It is a good thing to test yourself to see if you are growing and making progress. It is a good thing to test yourself against God's standards, to see if you are living in conformity to them. It's even helpful to be tested on knowledge, to see if you know the things you should know. Many churches have utilized catechisms for that very purpose. However, being tested to see how you compare with other people seems to me to be discouraged by Scripture (see Luke 18:9–14).

What Should My Children Know and When?

There are two different plumb lines we can consider when we are evaluating what our children need to know at what age. The first is the Bible, and the second is the State.

We are told, of the young Jesus:

> And Jesus grew in wisdom and stature, and in favor with God and man (Luke 2:52; NIV).

I think we can safely infer from this statement that there are objective units of measure that Jesus' parents used in His early life to keep tabs on His development and progress. There is wisdom in this. It is my contention that parents are generally the best people in the world to assess the strengths, weaknesses, and capabilities of their own children. No one knows the child better, or loves them more, than Mom and Dad.

Taking some basic guidelines found in Scripture, and some common sense, I think parents can, in most cases, adequately assess where their children are strong and where they are weak. There is no shame in using outside resources that may assist in that process (books on the topic of academic growth and development, for example). But in the end, I believe parents, not the government, should always be in the driver's seat when it comes to making educational decisions.

With that said, we live in a world where our government has encroached into nearly every sphere of our existence, including education, and many states have standards and requirements that they impose upon homeschoolers. With that in mind, I would again refer you to HSLDA.org for the requirements that may exist where you live, and to curriculum developers who have created materials to help you to know what the State thinks your child needs to know and when (scope and sequence for each "grade level").

Who Is Regulating Homeschoolers?

People sometimes say, "If there are no government regulations over homeschoolers (or not severe enough regulations), what will keep homeschoolers from just slacking off and doing nothing? How do we know that these children are learning what they should? How can we ensure homeschoolers are being properly educated?"

These arguments sound good on the surface, but are they logically sound? Consider this. Who keeps the government schools accountable to make sure that their students are learning and aren't falling behind academically?

There have been several court cases over the years in which parents sued their local school districts for an essential breach of contract, because their students had spent years in government school classrooms, and yet could not read.

Government Schools Do Not Promise to Educate Children!

On November 6, 2014, Judge Kathleen Jansen wrote the decision for Michigan Court of Appeals in a class action lawsuit against the Highland Park school system.

The defense of the school attorneys in several of these cases, and the agreement of the court on their behalf, was that it is impossible for a school to teach a student who does not get positive reinforcement at home. Judge Jansen claimed that you could encourage education, but not mandate it.[3]

She cited the earlier Michigan Supreme Court rule in *Milliken vs. Green*:

> It must be apparent by now that we are of the opinion that the state's obligation to provide a system of public schools is not the same as the claimed obligation to provide equality of educational opportunity. Because of definitional difficulties and differences in educational philosophy and student ability, motivation, background, etc., no system of public schools can provide equality of educational opportunity in all its diverse dimensions. All that can properly be expected of the state is that it maintains and supports a system of public schools that furnishes adequate educational services to all children.[4]

Do you hear what is being said here? The courts have determined that it is impossible for them to promise to *educate* children. They only promise to *school* them. Once again, this should remind us to never confuse schooling and education. They are *not* the same.

Additionally, in 1973, the U.S. Supreme Court ruled that, as important as it may be, education was not a fundamental right under the Constitution.[5] So schooling can be compulsory, but education is not.

In another case in California, a student had spent 12 years in government schools, and graduated when he was 18 without being able to read or write.[6]

In yet another case in New York, a student claimed that school officials had "failed to evaluate [his] mental ability and capacity to comprehend the subjects being taught to him at said school; failed to take proper means and precautions that they reasonably should have taken under the circumstances; failed to interview, discuss, evaluate and/or psychologically test [him] in order to ascertain his ability to comprehend and understand such matter; failed to provide adequate school facilities, teachers, administrators, psychologists, and other personnel trained to take the necessary steps in testing and evaluation processes insofar as [he] is concerned in order to ascertain the learning capacity, intelligence, and intellectual absorption on [his part]."[7]

The truth is, the government schools essentially have complete immunity when it comes to educational neglect. A homeschooler could, perceivably, be deemed guilty of educational neglect for having a child who is behind grade level. She could have her child taken away from her and placed in a government school. But what then? Who will force him to learn in that environment?

The hypocrisy of this system should be self-evident. When a homeschooler under-performs, the government schools claim it is the fault of the incompetent parents for trying to educate their children at home. And when government school students under-perform, the schools claim it is the fault of the parents, who are not doing enough to help their student at home. It's a "heads I win, tails you lose" situation.

It is true that a school or teacher could be threatened with economic sanctions of some kind if the government school students under-perform. But this does not guarantee that those children will be properly educated.

Education Cannot Be Forced

In the end, if a student does not want to learn, no one can force that child to learn. Conversely, if a student wants to learn, you cannot keep that child from learning. Look at the dozens of examples we have in American History alone of individuals who had very little formal schooling, and yet went on to do great things, even becoming president of the United States.

If a child does not have reinforcement from the parents (resulting in a student who is below grade level), that same student will likely under-perform in the government school classroom as well. There will always be students who have learning difficulties. There will always be students who have no desire to learn. That's a reality that must be accepted. This concept of forced equality is not a biblical idea, but rather, it comes out of a socialistic mindset. It is my contention that students (in a worst-case scenario) who are staying at home, learning very little, because they have no desire to learn, is better off than the student who is forced to attend a school. The uninterested school student is also learning little or nothing, but is doing so at a cost of well over $10,000 per year to taxpayers. In the end, compulsory attendance laws will never force a single person to want to learn. Providing a safe, welcoming, encouraging, and loving learning environment in the home has the best chance of accomplishing the objective of creating a life-long love for learning.

Endnotes

1. John Taylor Gatto, *The Underground History of American Education* (Oxford, NY: The Oxford Village Press, 2001), p. 379–380.
2. Ibid.
3. ACLU vs. Highland Park, http://cases.justia.com/michigan/court-of-appeals-published/2014-317071-2.pdf?ts=1415365369.
4. Ibid.
5. *San Antonio Independent School District v. Rodriguez*, 411 U.S. 1 (1973).
6. *Peter W. v. San Francisco Unified Sch. District* (1976).
7. *Donohue v. Copiague UFSD*, 47 N.Y.2d 440 (1979).

CHAPTER 6

What about Socialization?

Even after all these years, the socialization question is one of the most common that homeschoolers face. There are two presuppositions that are embedded in this question. The first relates to outcome; the second relates to methods or means.

The first assumption is that if students are not properly socialized, they will not be good citizens as adults. They will not know how to communicate with, and relate to, others.

The second assumption is that the only viable means to create a good student is to enroll him or her in an institutional school classroom (of 20–40 students), in which everyone is the same age.

Is Peer Group Socialization Biblical?

Where did this idea of institutional classroom learning as a means to proper socialization come from? I can assure you, it did not come from the Bible. In Proverbs 13:20 (NKJV), we are warned, "He who walks with wise men will be wise, but the companion of fools will be destroyed."

This is a very stern warning! If this is true (and we know it is because it is God's Word), then we must be diligent, as parents, to avoid the companionship of fools. But what is a fool? The Bible gives us two clear definitions, and both are found in a government school classroom!

The first is in Psalm 53:1a where it says, "The fool says in his heart, 'There is no God.' "

The second is found in Proverbs 22:15, which teaches, "Folly is bound up in the heart of a child."

Therefore, you must avoid having your children taught in an educational system that insists that God does not exist or is irrelevant. Remember, an irrelevant God is the same as no God at all. It is fascinating to me that Christian parents actively seek out groups of foolish children and teachers, who deny or minimize the importance of God, to serve as companions for their offspring.

First Corinthians 15:33 informs us, "Do not be deceived: 'Bad company ruins good morals.' "

Social Education Theory

Peer dependency is an essential ingredient in government schooling. Radical progressive social engineers like John Dewey knew that if you created a classroom of children, all the same age, in one year's time the majority of the students would shift their allegiance from their parents to their peers. Thus, Karl Marx proudly proclaimed in the *Communist Manifesto*, "(W)e destroy the most hallowed of relations when we replace home education by social."[1]

Influence is determined by two primary factors:

1. Time
2. Affirmation

Whoever spends the most time with a child and affirms him or her the most will have the most influence in the child's life. As parents, you should desire for that position of influence to belong to you, not to your child's peer group. Social engineers who want to take cultures in a leftist, socialist, "progressive" direction have always sought to get children away from their parents so they could gain influence and dominance over entire generations. Government school systems have been key in this process.

Won't They Miss Their Friends in School?

As parents, we need to know who our child's friends are, what they are doing, and hopefully be with them as they interact with their friends. The goal is not to isolate our children and keep them away from all other children, but we should not assume that all childhood friendships are going to be positive (they are not!).

In an institutional school setting, children are forced to interact with many children who will be negative influences. In a homeschooling setting, parents can choose social contexts that, hopefully, will be more positive. Homeschooled children often interact with other children in homeschool groups (co-ops, sports teams, music bands, drama clubs, etc.), church, and other community and family settings. Most homeschoolers are far from isolated. And even those who are isolated because of geography or other reasons, usually end up being completely socially adjusted in their adult years.

If you have a large family like ours, you have a built-in social group for your child. Our children are never lonely! They always have a buddy with whom they can play and do activities together. If you are the parent of an only child, you may need to be more intentional about finding social activities at church, through your homeschool support group, or with other likeminded friends.

How Will They Make Friends?

"A man of many companions may come to ruin, but there is a friend who sticks closer than a brother" (Prov. 18:24). Good friends are hard to find. The Bible discourages the concept of sending our children into large groups of unwise children, but encourages the development of godly friendships. If someone wants to have friends, they need to learn to show themselves to be friendly. I believe a great way for your children to get to know, and spend time with, other children is to invite other families into your home. Rather than sending your children away from your home to spend time with their peers apart from your super-vision, getting to know entire family units provides friendship and accountability.

Friendships for children have value, but their importance should never be placed above the unity of the family itself.

Will My Child Be Socially Awkward?

Some people really struggle with interacting with others. This is a personality issue, not a schooling issue. If someone is an introvert, he or she will be an introvert at school as well. If someone is an extrovert, he or she will love interacting with people even though he or she is homeschooled. I know hundreds of socially awkward people who graduated from government schools. Being in a school is not a cure for awkwardness. If you have a child who struggles with social interaction, you need to work with that child and help the child to overcome his or her fears, bad habits, and/or inhibitions.

At 14 years old, I had my own radio show. I would go to malls and teen hangouts and interview my fellow teenagers on cultural issues. I've always been a social person. I make my living traveling around the country speaking at conferences to tens of thousands of people every year. Homeschooling didn't hinder me in any way regarding my interactions with others. I will say, however, that on the other hand, the two years I spent in private Christian school (2nd and 6th grade) were absolute disasters for me. I was too social! I got in trouble for all my socializing during school hours!

In the end, the research has proven that homeschooled adults are more socially engaged and contributing more positively to their communities than their traditionally schooled counterparts.

Can Our Children Spend Too Much Time with Us?

Again, time and affirmation equal influence. How much influence do you want to have with your children? How much influence do you want other people to have, especially when they are working against your influence? Most children do not resent time spent with their parents or their siblings unless that time is notably negative. If parents are frequently frustrated, angry, and stressed out, then children will desire to be elsewhere, interacting with non-family members.

It is important to remember that relationships need to trump academics. If relationships are in place, you will have influence. If you have influence, you can teach. If you lose influence, you can't teach or motivate effectively.

If your child loves time away from you and always desires social activities that do not include the family, I think it is time to do a relational checkup. Perhaps you need to take time to build relationally by just having fun with your children.

Conformity in the Classroom

In the 1950s, a social psychologist named Solomon Asch began conducting conformity experiments in university classrooms. Control groups were created, and students were instructed to give false answers to obvious questions. Only one student in the group would be unaware that he or she was part of a social experiment. It was found that the power of the peer group was very strong, even at the university level, where students believed that giving the correct answer was imperative to receive a passing grade. About three-quarters of the group showed some susceptibility to peer pressure and altered their answers to conform to the consensus of the group (even when they knew they were giving the wrong answer).[2]

The two main reasons given by the students for why they gave the wrong answers, when they knew the basic and obvious correct ones, were:

1. They didn't want to be ridiculed by the rest of the class.
2. They questioned their own sanity.

The power of popular opinion is persuasive to us, even as adults. How much more would it be for small children or junior high students who desire (even more than life in some cases) to fit in and be accepted by their friends and peers.

Far from being a reason to choose government schooling, the socialization question should be one of the primary reasons we choose homeschooling for our children. We want them to find love and acceptance in their family, their extended family, their local church, and carefully selected friends who will be a positive influence. We don't want them to be thrown into a situation where they are pressured into foolishness and ungodly behavior by teachers and students who do not share our faith and values.

Endnotes

1. Marx & Engels, *The Communist Manifesto*, "Chapter II. Proletarians and Communists" (1848).
2. https://www.simplypsychology.org/asch-conformity.html.

CHAPTER 7

Isn't Sheltering a Child Harmful?

Because of the bullying that children experience and observe in their schools, many parents are choosing to homeschool. In Washington state, one homeschool support group reported that approximately 1/3 of the families in their group had chosen homeschooling to protect their students from classroom threats. For many students growing up between 1950 and 1969, bullying was a part of childhood. No one enjoyed being the victim of harassment, but at the same time, very few people thought it was outside of the bounds of expected behavior for youth.[1] Lunch money was often confiscated by school thugs. Youth would be pushed off the sidewalk, called names, cursed at, etc.

If you were a male, you probably didn't tell your parents when you were bullied, and if you did, your dad likely told you, "Stop being a sissy. You need to toughen up and be a man."

Times have changed. After the Columbine school shooting on April 20, 1999, America will probably never again simply shrug off aggressive or threatening behavior from students as a "normal" part of life.

Today, bullying includes a degree of aggressiveness that was rare or unheard of in the 1950s and '60s. Sexual assault; cyber-bullying;[2] stalking, threatening with harm; stealing personal items; being called degrading, sexually oriented names;

etc., are common occurrences for many youths in government schools.

Nearly 1 in 3 students (27.8 percent) report being bullied during the school year (National Center for Educational Statistics, 2013).[3] According to NoBullying.com, 70.6 percent of teens have seen bullying occur in their schools. Many victims have reported such activities to school authorities, only to find that they often do nothing, or respond with a one-day suspension, which does nothing to decrease the ongoing assaults against weaker students.

Parenting and Protecting

When children arrive in this world, they are completely helpless and reliant on their parents for care and protection. Sheltering your children is an innate part of parenting young children.

Protection for the innocent and oppressed (specifically for family members) is outlined in the Bible in Psalm 41:1; Isaiah 1:17; Jeremiah 22:16; 1 Timothy 5:8; James 1:27; and others.

It is the Christian's duty to ensure that no one is ever unjustly attacked when it is within our power to intervene. It is love that motivates someone to protect. Defending another person, even at risk of peril to one's own safety, is described by Christ as the supreme expression of love.

> Greater love hath no man than this, that a man lay down his life for his friends (John 15:13; KJV).

Parents have a responsibility to keep their children safe from truly harmful influences, especially those that are morally corrupting and damaging to the soul.

Over-protecting?

Things that are appropriate in balance can become harmful or destructive when they reach imbalance. The same is true with protecting your children. Sociologists talk about "helicopter parents" who "hover" over their children to ensure that nothing bad happens to them. Even college deans get calls from these over-protective parents when their children get bad grades or are disciplined by the school. These parents insist that Johnny needs to be given special treatment and that he is misunderstood. Some parents even end up doing all their children's homework assignments to ensure they make good grades and don't lose opportunities (apparently neglecting to remember that their children may actually need to know some of these skills themselves when they get into the workforce).

To become strong, you must face some resistance in life. It is the weight of opposition that builds both physical muscles and godly character. If a parent constantly carries the burden for his child, he is setting that child up to fail in life.

I've heard some parents say, "Homeschooling is bad for children because it prevents them from being bullied. They need to get beat up a few times in life to know how to handle the real world." Personally, I'm not okay with that worldview, but there is wisdom needed in knowing how to keep a proper balance on these issues.

We don't need to intentionally place our children in harm's way, but neither should we seek to shelter them from the natural consequences of their own choices and actions. Especially if they have chosen to participate in foolish behavior, or have blatantly disregarded wisdom, we need to allow the weight of their choices to rest on their own shoulders.

When I was a teen, there was a young man (a "tweener") in our church who was a bully to many of the younger children at the church. Church staff who worked in the children's ministry would often try to speak to the parents about their son's behavior. Unfortunately, the parents never believed the other adults. They insisted that their child would never behave like that. They accused the church staff of picking on, and even bullying, their son! When concerns continued to be raised, the parents eventually left the church, feeling offended and wrongly persecuted.

That young man was quickly learning how to "work the system." He knew that his parents would defend him and bail him out whenever he got in trouble. That type of scenario often continues into the teen and young adult years when Dad perpetually bails out Junior from jail and pays off his debts.

Finding Balance

To parent properly, we need to truly know our children. One way we do this is by listening objectively to the assessments of our children by others who spend time them with them when we aren't present.

We must remember, "Train up a child in the way he should go; even when he is old he will not depart from it" (Prov. 22:6).

Our job as parents is not merely to keep externally harmful influences away from our children, but it is also to seek to deal with the deception and foolishness that dwells *inside* of them. Rather than having a default position that would believe that "our little angel would NEVER do something like that," we should seek to learn the truth. It is the truth that sets us (and our children) free.

James 1:19 says, "Know this, my beloved brothers: let every person be quick to hear, slow to speak, slow to anger."

This is the posture we must take as parents. We need to carefully listen and be slow to make a judgment. Sometimes we believe that bad behavior on the part of our child reflects negatively on us or our parenting. Therefore, it is easy to simply dismiss the problem as being imagined rather than face up to the reality. If, through prayerful consideration, it becomes clear that we have been enabling our children in bad behavior, we need to be willing to make necessary changes to correct the situation.

What to Do?

1. Protect Your Child

If your child describes a situation in which he or she has been a victim of bullying, please take the situation seriously. Many children and teens have chosen to take their lives when they feel they have no advocate and proper protection from ongoing harm and intimidation. Keep them away from social environments and social media where there is just reason to believe negative activity is taking place.

2. Teach Your Child to Protect Others Rather Than Cause Harm

Stopping bullying begins with parents teaching their children right from wrong. Teach your children to be defenders of the weak and oppressed and to never use a position of strength or power to impose harm on others.

3. Be Willing to Consider Accusations Against Your Child

While you shouldn't assume that your child is always in the wrong if an accusation is placed on him or her by another youth or adult, you also should never assume he or she would never be guilty of wrong. All children have sinful hearts and a tendency to do what they should not. Proper parenting will seek opportunities to help your child learn from his mistakes and to make restitution whenever possible.

4. Lead by Example

Children learn more by watching our example than they do by listening to our words. The best way to ensure that we are not raising a bully, but rather are raising a godly protector and peacemaker, is to become those things ourselves. We should create a climate or atmosphere of peace and justice. We should constantly seek peace and pursue it (see Psalm 34:14; Hebrews 12:14; and 1 Peter 3:11). Our desire is to be an appropriate shade and shelter for our children until they can eventually become the same for others.

If possible, so far as it depends on you, live peaceably with all (Rom. 12:18).

Endnotes
1. Steven Arthur Provis, "Bullying (1950 - 2010): The Bully and the Bullied" (2012), Dissertations, 381, http://ecommons.luc.edu/luc_diss/381.

2. The 2013 *Youth Risk Behavior Surveillance Survey* finds that 15 percent of high school students (grades 9–12) were electronically bullied in the past year. Source: StopBullying.gov.

3. nces.ed.gov.

CHAPTER 8

What about Being Salt and Light in Public School?

The prevailing view among evangelicals today is that we need to send our children into government-run schools for them to "be salt and light." I address this issue extensively in my book *Education: Does God Have an Opinion? A Biblical Apologetic for Christian Education & Homeschooling.* See the chapter "What about Government Schooling?" for a more systematic treatise on this topic.

How Was Jesus Educated?

There is no evidence to suggest that Jesus was ever schooled outside the home. The first time that Jesus emerged on the scene as a talking, reasoning young man, He was 12 years old. He accompanied His family to Jerusalem for the Passover feast. He ended up heading to the temple and engaging the rabbis with questions. "After three days, they found him in the temple, sitting among the teachers, listening to them and asking them questions" (Luke 2:46). Upon being discovered by His parents, He submitted to them and returned home with them.

There are a few things we can infer from this account in Luke 2.

First, we can see that Jesus' desire to learn had not been squelched. Often, institutional schooling creates an apathy for discovery and learning that is difficult to refuel. Jesus' education, up to that point, had obviously been a positive experience.

Second, we see that Jesus had learned how to think and to ask good questions. He was not a passive learner. He knew *how* to learn. He knew where to go to find the information He was seeking.

Third, it is obvious that He loved the Scripture. That is rare for a 12-year-old boy. This reflects, I believe, a proper emphasis His parents placed on the most important things.

Did Jesus Go to School?

It is sometimes argued that most Hebrew boys during Jesus' lifetime attended Hebraic schools. Nothing in Scripture tells us this, and I find the historical evidence to substantiate this rather sketchy.

We do know that Yehoshua ben Gamla, or Joshua son of Gamaliel, a Jewish high priest around A.D. 64 advocated for formal schooling for boys. The Talmud tells us: "At first every father had to teach his children. A large school was then opened in Jerusalem; and after that schools were established in every community. At first, they were attended only by youths of sixteen or seventeen years; but Joshua b. Gamla introduced the custom that children of six or seven years should attend the schools: interesting regulations are added concerning the location of public schools, the number of pupils for each class, and the like."[1]

This was really just a short time before the destruction of Jerusalem in A.D. 70, so it appears to me that this practice was rather short-lived. Joshua was not the son of Gamaliel (the Pharisee) who tutored the young Saul of Tarsus. I have found no solid evidence that most male students under 16 were being taught in formal schools, in any culturally dominant way, during the childhood of Jesus.

However, even if that was true, there is no indication that Jesus attended. More importantly, even if Jesus *did* attend such a school (which is very doubtful in my mind, as I believe Scripture would speak to the matter in that case), it would have been one that emphasized the *Tenakh* (the Hebrew Old Testament), rather than the Greco-Roman myths and philosophies.

Jesus' parents clearly didn't send Him to a pagan school to be educated in the beliefs and practices of the heathens. If that was the goal for God's children, don't you think Jesus' family would have tried to follow the best model for Jesus? If any child was equipped to be able to stand up against error and confront the falsehood of the day, it surely would have been Jesus! But rather than send Him to a pagan (or "secular") school, they chose an education that emphasized Scripture as the core of His learning.

Jesus did not begin His public ministry, refuting opponents and battling for truth in the public square, until He was 30 years old. Surely, this is instructive for us. Young children are not equipped to be able to stand against the false ideas presented by grown adults (whom they are instructed to honor and learn from) and the pressure from herds of peers.

The Pagan World at the Time of Jesus

One of the leading historians on the Jewish culture during the life of Jesus, Alfred Edersheim, says of the culture outside of Israel:

> Strange as it may sound, it is strictly true that, beyond the boundaries of Israel, it would be scarcely possible to speak with any propriety of family life, or even of the family, as we understand these terms. It is significant, that the Roman historian Tacitus should mark it as something special among the Jews — which they only shared with the ancient barbarian Germans — that they regarded it as a crime to kill their offspring!
>
> This is not the place to describe the exposure of children, or the various crimes by which ancient Greece and Rome, in the days of their highest culture, sought to rid themselves of what was regarded as superfluous population. Few of those who have learned to admire classical antiquity have a full conception of any one phase in its social life — whether of the position of woman, the relation of the sexes, slavery, the education of children, their relation to their parents, or the state of public morality.[2]

The secular culture of Jesus' day was every bit as morally decadent as (or worse than!) ours. It was surely a day in which the pagans needed to be evangelized. Yet Joseph and Mary didn't choose pagan schooling for their son. In contrast to a heathen education, listen to how Edersheim describes the mindset behind a God-fearing, Jewish home education:

> When we pass from the heathen world into the homes of Israel, even the excess of their exclusiveness seems for the moment a relief. It is as if we turned from enervating, withering, tropical heat into a darkened room, whose grateful coolness makes us for the moment forget that its gloom is excessive, and cannot continue as the day declines. And this shutting out of all from without, this exclusiveness, applied not only to what concerned their religion, their social and family life, but also to their knowledge. In the days of Christ, the pious Jew had no other knowledge, neither sought nor cared for any other — in fact, denounced it — than that of the law of God. At the outset, let it be remembered that, in heathenism, theology, or rather mythology, had no influence whatever on thinking or life — was literally submerged under their waves. To the pious Jew, on the contrary, the knowledge of God was everything; and to prepare for or impart that knowledge was the sum total, the sole object of his education. This was the life of his soul — the better, and only true life, to which all else as well as the life of the body were merely subservient, as means towards an end.[3]

Shouldn't our mentality be that of Jesus' parents, who sought the knowledge of God as being our primary focus? Surely no one will argue that Jesus was too sheltered to make any impact on the world. Surely no one will criticize His parents for giving Him instruction that was saturated in the holy Scriptures. Surely no one will accuse them of being negligent in their duties by keeping Him from being exposed to "the real world."

Evangelism in Context

The Jewish model of education did not focus on mere academic instruction, but also on life application. Biblical scholar Emil Schürer says of the education Jesus would have received:

> (B)oth the knowledge and practice of the law were required. Josephus boasts of it as an excellence of the Israelitish nation, that in their case, neither one nor the other received a one-sided preference, as in the case of the Spartans, who educated by custom, not by instruction, and neglected practice. "But our lawgiver very carefully combined the two. For he neither left the practice of morals silent, nor the teaching of the law unperformed."[4]

Jesus is the one who told us that we are salt and light (Matt. 5:13–14). Jesus was *the* "light of the world" (John 8:12). He was the example we should all follow. The reason Jesus was so effective in His ministry was because He lived in contrast to the darkness. He wasn't assimilated into the darkness. When Jesus' public work of evangelism began at the age of 30, He was prepared. He was equipped and ready. Even though He knew His calling at the age of 12, He wasn't ready yet. He needed more time and more preparation. This should be instructive for us as we seek to raise our children to follow in Jesus' footsteps.

Endnotes

1. Baba Batra 21a, "The Last Gate," http://jewishencyclopedia.com/articles/2274-baba-batra.
2. Alfred Edersheim, *Sketches of Jewish Social Life in the Days of Christ*, chapter 8 (1876): "Subjects of Study. Home Education in Israel; Female Education. Elementary Schools, Schoolmasters, and School Arrangements," http://biblehub.com/library/edersheim/sketches_of_jewish_social_life/chapter_8_subjects_of_study.htm.
3. Ibid.
4. Josephus (an ancient Jewish Historian), *Contra Apion*, ii, 16–17; Emil Schürer, D.D., M.A., *A History of the Jewish People in the Time of Jesus Christ*, Second Division, Vol. II (Peabody, MA: Hendrickson Publishers. Originally published by T & T Clark: Edinburgh, 1890), p. 45–46.

CHAPTER 9

Is Homeschooling Elitist?

Over the many years that I've been involved in the home education movement, I have heard the accusation, on occasion,
that homeschooling is elitist or separationist. Is that true? Do
people home educate their children because they believe their
children are better than others?

For me personally, I have never heard anyone say they are
homeschooling because they want to create an attitude of superiority in their children. In all the studies on home education, I've
never seen elitism listed as a motivation for why someone wants
to homeschool.

Is it possible, however, that this might motivate some parents,
even subconsciously, or at least privately? Could it be something
they believe, but know they shouldn't talk about publicly?

Consider what the Association of California School Administrators wrote:

> "Parent choice" proceeds from the belief that the pur-
> pose of education is to provide individual students with
> an education. In fact, educating the individual is but a
> means to the true end of education, which is to create a
> viable social order to which individuals contribute and
> by which they are sustained. "Family choice" is, there-
> fore, basically selfish and anti-social in that it focuses on
> the "wants" of a single family rather than the "needs" of
> society.[1]

Wait a minute! Parents who want a choice in the education of their children are selfish and anti-social? I think it is ironic that people who speak the loudest against "judging," and the need to "be tolerant," are usually the most intolerant, judgmental people on the planet.

Is it Wrong to Be Elitist?

There are several presuppositions behind this question. One of them is that it is important for children, who are raised in a certain society, to grow up being tolerant and accepting of others who are not like them. It is also assumed that these children should grow up and become assimilated into the culture, becoming good, productive citizens who contribute positively to the well-being and economy of their communities.

There is a dominant and prevailing egalitarian worldview in our country that all people are created equal in worth and value. This is a Christian perspective as well. However, some go so far as to say society should create mechanisms to maintain a forced equality, both socially and economically (hence an increasing acceptance of socialism, as a great equalizer, for the common good).

In Germany, homeschooling is illegal. The German government's current compulsory attendance laws (which were established by Adolf Hitler) insist that all children have a "right" to a secular, LGBT, government-controlled education. This "right" is so fundamental and dominant that you don't have the "right" to opt out of it. Creating a system where no one has freedom of choice is of great benefit to the elites who control the government. Those who speak against the elitism of family-controlled education have no qualms against the elitism of government-controlled education. The irony is thick.

Is the "Melting Pot" of Pluralism a Good Idea?

If we go back to the time of the Israelites, we see many scriptural admonitions to God's people that they were to be separate and distinct from the nations around them. The terms "holiness" and "sanctified" both have connotations of being "set apart" *from* the ways of the pagan culture, and *to* the Lord.

> You shall make no covenant with them and their gods. They shall not dwell in your land, lest they make you sin against me; for if you serve their gods, it will surely be a snare to you (Exod. 23:32–33).

Even in the New Testament, God's people are called to separation and distinction.

> Do not be unequally yoked with unbelievers. For what partnership has righteousness with lawlessness? Or what fellowship has light with darkness? What accord has Christ with Belial? Or what portion does a believer share with an unbeliever? What agreement has the temple of God with idols? For we are the temple of the living God; as God said, "I will make my dwelling among them and walk among them, and I will be their God, and they shall be my people. Therefore go out from their midst, and be separate from them, says the Lord, and touch no unclean thing; then I will welcome you, and I will be a father to you, and you shall be sons and daughters to me, says the Lord Almighty" (2 Cor. 6:14–18).

Does this give Christians license to abandon society and live secluded lives, avoiding all contact with non-Christians? Do people choose to homeschool because they look down on people who aren't like them, and want to prevent their children from exposure to, or interaction with, those who aren't of their "tribe"?

In the World, Not of It

It seems that the primary emphasis in the New Testament, regarding the issue of separation from the world, is one of beliefs, values, and worldviews. There is a certain philosophy of life that is embraced, and pursued, by those who do not walk in submission to Christ, and we are to avoid that humanistic way of living (that puts mankind at the center of the proverbial universe).

Paul warns us to be separate in our thinking, and in our actions and lifestyle as well.

> Now this I say and testify in the Lord, that you must no longer walk as the Gentiles do, *in the futility of their minds* (Eph. 4:17, emphasis added).

> Do not be conformed to this world, *but be transformed by the renewal of your mind*, that by testing you may discern what is the will of God, what is good and acceptable and perfect (Rom. 12:2, emphasis added).

Does this mean that we should have nothing to do with unbelievers? No, it does not. In fact, the opposite is true. Jesus called us "salt" and "light," "a city on a hill." We aren't to be hidden under a bushel.

The question is not whether Christians should live in the world and interact with non-Christians. That is a given. We live in the world. The real question is regarding the nature of that interaction.

> I have given them your word, and the world has hated them because they are not of the world, just as I am not of the world. I do not ask that you take them out of the world, but that you keep them from the evil one. They are not of the world, just as I am not of the world. Sanctify them in the truth; your word is truth. As you sent me into the world, so I have sent them into the world. And for their sake I consecrate myself, that they also may be sanctified in truth. I do not ask for these only, but also for those who will believe in me through their word (John 17:14–20).

War of the Worldviews

Truth is, by definition, exclusive. When you claim that something is true, the Law of Non-Contradiction (in formal logic) insists that the opposite of any such claim (a thesis) is, by necessity, false (an antithesis). The government school system teaches truth is relative, macro-evolution is the cause of all living things, and sexual ethics are whatever we want them to be. These views are not compatible with the teachings of the Bible. These ideas, and their antithesis, cannot all hold equal weight and value. Someone is right, and someone else is wrong. When homeschoolers say that they do not agree with, and do not wish to participate in, things they consider to be immoral or untrue, this is not elitism. Rather it is a necessary position for any intellectually honest person. The government school system makes no qualms about saying those who oppose their goals and agenda are wrong. As Christian homeschoolers, we do not believe our children are innately better than anyone else. In fact, the Doctrine of Original Sin insists that everyone is born with an inclination to sin and disobedience. We are aware of this, and it motivates us to ensure that our child's education is centered on the gospel.

Is Public School Elitist?

I think an argument can be made, based on its history and practice, that the government school system is predicated on the belief that it is the best form of schooling for children. To claim something is "better" is to make a value judgment. To claim something is "the best" opens itself up to the potential accusation of elitism, does it not? So why would homeschoolers be deemed elitist, but government schools not, when they equally claim that the approach they are taking, and the content of their information, is "the best"?

The National Education Association (NEA) has expressed its view that government education is superior to home education:

> The National Education Association believes that home schooling programs based on parental choice cannot provide the student with a comprehensive education experience.[2]

Especially in the face of the academic excellence, and positive societal contributions from the majority of home-educated students, is this not mere unsubstantiated, elitist bias?

The Gospel — The Great Equalizer

Christianity teaches that we are born equally sinful (Rom. 3:23). No Christian has a reason to be boastful on the basis of our innate goodness (we have none), or even their intellectual superiority. We are warned against knowledge that puffs up (1Cor. 8:1). Being homeschooled does not save you. It does not make you more holy. Homeschooling is a context. It is a learning environment that is the most conducive to parent-directed Christian discipleship.

Some ideas are superior to others. Some teaching methods are superior to others. Some social situations are less desirable than others. This is not elitism. This is merely common sense and inescapable reality.

Young, impressionable children need to be raised in a culture where they are sheltered from harmful influences in their most formative years. The reason is so they will have a strong sense of their own identity (hopefully grounded in a personal relationship with Christ) and can then reach out in love to others around them.

Endnotes

1. Association of California School Administrators (ACSA, October 1979), Ref: Policy Issues for the 1990s by Ray C. Rist, page 738; also see *Presbyterian Journal*, December 5, 1979).
2. http://www.nea.org/assets/docs/nea-resolutions-2014-15.pdf.

CHAPTER 10

Will Homeschoolers Be Good Citizens?

Closely linked to the "What about socialization?" question is the "good citizen" question. It is assumed that if children do not attend government schools, they will not know how to grow up and relate to other people in the "real world."

How did this line of thinking originate, and is there any truth to it?

Where Did It All Begin?

From the very beginning of the government schooling system, both in America and Europe, powerful social engineers envisioned a brave new world, in which entire nations could be reshaped and refashioned into a socialistic, new world order.

New Social Order

It was Karl Marx, in *The Communist Manifesto,* who talked about the need to "replace home education by social." Vladimir Lenin envisioned a world where many "useful idiots" would unquestionably do the bidding of the powerful, and where society could be transformed into a new image. He declared:

> The school, apart from life, apart from politics, is a lie, a hypocrisy. Bourgeois society indulged in this lie, covering up the fact that it was using the schools as a means of

domination, by declaring that the school was politically neutral, and in the service of all. We must declare openly what it concealed, namely, the political function of the school. While the object of our previous struggle was to overthrow the bourgeoisie (the middle class), the aim of the new generation is much more complex: It is to construct communist society.[1]

He also stated in his speech at the First All-Russian Educational Congress, August 28, 1918: "We say that our work in the sphere of education is part of the struggle for the overthrow of the bourgeoisie. We publicly declare that education divorced from life and politics is a lie and hypocrisy."[2]

The following is from William L. Shirer's *The Rise and Fall of the Third Reich*:

[Adolf Hitler] had stressed in his book the importance of winning over and then training the youth in the service "of a new national state" — a subject he returned to often after he became the German dictator. "When an opponent declares, 'I will not come over to your side,' [Hitler] said in a speech on November 6, 1933, 'I calmly say, "Your child belongs to us already. . . . What are you? You will pass on. Your descendants, however, now stand in the new camp. In a short time, they will know nothing else but this new community.'" And on May 1, 1937, [Hitler] declared, "This new Reich will give its youth to no one, but will itself take youth and give to youth its own education and its own upbringing." It was not an idle boast; that was precisely what was happening. The German schools, from first grade through the universities, were quickly Nazified.[3]

These social engineers recognized that if you want to steer the ship in a new direction, you'd need to first get children away from their parents, and then start the process of "re-education," or indoctrination. John Dewey, the father of the socialistic Progressive Education Movement, admitted this openly:

The work of the schools finds its meaning expressed in words one often hears: "Nothing can be done with the older generation as a whole. Its 'ideology' was fixed by the older régime; we can only wait for them to die. Our positive hope is in the younger generation."[4]

The "Right" Kind of Citizen

What is the "right" kind of citizen? The desire of the "progressives" was to create a citizen who was Marxist in their economics, atheist or agnostic in their theology, and relativistic in their ethics. They have accomplished their goals with astounding definiteness.

In 1932, American Communist leader William Z. Foster prophesied the establishment of a National Department of Education to enable the schools to create a new social order:

> Among the elementary measures the American Soviet government will adopt to further the revolution are the following; the schools and colleges will be coordinated and grouped under the National Department of Education and its state and local branches. The studies will be revolutionized, being cleansed of religious, patriotic, and other features of the bourgeois ideology. The students will be taught on the basis of Marxian dialectical materialism, internationalism, and general ethics of the new Socialist society.[5]

This goal was not realized until 1979, when then President Jimmy Carter was finally able to enact this "progressive" dream of national statist schooling.

The thing you need to realize is that the agenda behind government-controlled education has been advancing slowly since its very inception. The American government school system did not start out Christian and then sort of "lose its way." It was predicated on the promotion of the religion of humanism. This is the belief that mankind is the measure of all things, and we don't need God in society to tell us right from wrong. We can decide for ourselves what we should do. This is the lie that the serpent told Eve in the garden, and people have fallen for it ever since.

So, when we ask the question, "Will homeschoolers be good citizens?" we must, by necessity, define some terms. What do we mean by "good citizen"?

What Is a "Good Citizen"?

The Marxist / Leninist worldview teaches that the purpose of an education is to create a non-questioning citizen who will serve the purposes of the government (nationally or internationally). The Christian worldview says that the purpose of an education is to glorify God and to be equipped to love and serve your neighbor in practical ways.

Academics are a means for preparing a young person for life. It gives them knowledge, skills, and abilities that they can use to either serve the state (Marxism), themselves (humanism), or God and others (Christianity).

When viewed through Christian lenses, it becomes crucial to help to cultivate students who have not bought into the "party line." We want students who are truly educated (not merely schooled), who can think for themselves, and who aren't afraid to go against the norm and question the status quo. The individualism cultivated in a home learning environment is most consistent with that goal. At the same time, however, we don't want to create students who only think for, and about, themselves. We want them to truly love and care for others. That is why I advocate for Christian homeschooling (not merely homeschooling).

Following, then, this Christian definition, we would hope to see a person who:

1. Knows what he/she believes (has convictions)
2. Stays informed about social and cultural issues
3. Is willing to speak or write on important civic issues and causes
4. Votes in local, state, and national elections

5. Helps to elect candidates who will protect and defend the Constitution
6. Donates time and money to charitable causes
7. Gives back to the community in positive ways
8. Regularly participates in a local church
9. Financially supports himself/herself and his/her family
10. Pays taxes required by law
11. Does not engage in illegal, immoral, or unethical activity
12. Feels satisfied in life

In 2007, the Home School Legal Defense Association (HSLDA) commissioned a study conducted by Dr. Brian Ray of students who had been home educated, but were now adults, living in the "real world." Over 7,300 homeschooled graduates participated. Over 5,000 of them had been homeschooled for seven years or more. The study, entitled *Homeschooling Grows Up*, indicated definitively that homeschoolers were, at every measurable benchmark, more positively engaged with society than their governmentally schooled counterparts.[6]

Homeschoolers are more likely to:

Obtain a college degree, read books, stay abreast of important news items, attend religious services, volunteer for community service, give a speech or write in defense of their values, understand law and government, vote in political elections, vote for candidates, give money to political campaigns, etc.

Homeschoolers tend to be successfully employed in a wide array of occupations. They are more satisfied with life than students raised in government schools, and only 2.1 percent agreed, even nominally, that homeschooling hindered them in any way or limited their career choice; and 92.4 percent agreed that being home educated provided a definite advantage for them as adults.

So, the myth about homeschoolers not being good citizens is just that. The problem that the progressives have with homeschooling is that it does not tend to produce the predictable, unquestioning, politically correct citizens for which they aim.

Has there ever been an antisocial homeschooled student who did something stupid or illegal or immoral and embarrassed his family? Of course. When you have well over two million homeschooled students (as we do today), there are bound to be a few bad apples. But the data is clear: homeschoolers, by an overwhelming majority, are excellent citizens by every possible positive benchmark.

Endnotes

1. John Dewey quoted Lenin in *Impressions of Soviet Russia and the Revolutionary World*, 1929, from the chapter "What are the Russian Schools Doing?" http://ariwatch.com/VS/JD/ImpressionsOfSovietRussia.htm#chapter4.
2. Ibid.
3. William Shirer, *Rise and Fall of the Third Reich* (New York: Simon and Schuster, 1960), 249.
4. Ibid. Dewey, from the chapter, "A New World in the Making."
5. William Z. Foster, *Toward Soviet America* (New York, NY: Coward-McCann, Inc., 1932), p. 316, https://archive.org/details/towardsovietamer00fostrich.
6. Dr. Brian Ray, *Homeschooling Grows Up* (2007), https://www.hslda.org/research/ray2003/default.asp.

CHAPTER 11

What If I Don't Have Enough Patience?

" I could never homeschool my children. I don't have enough patience. I couldn't stand to have them around me that much!" Have you ever heard those lines? What about, "I can't wait for the school year to start! It will be such a relief to have the children back in school. They are driving me crazy!"

I can't tell you how often I've heard these sentiments expressed. Many parents even say such things within earshot of their children.

Whenever a parent says something like that to me, my immediate response is, "Well, I guess that you, even more than other parents, really need to homeschool your children!" This always results in dropped jaws and incredulous stares.

Doesn't It Cause Conflict with Your Kids When You Are Their Teacher?

There are two main reasons that God wants you to take responsibility for the discipleship of your children. The first reason has nothing to do with your children. That's right! As counter-intuitive as it sounds, God wants you to teach your children for a purpose that doesn't relate to them or their needs.

You see, whether we like to admit it or not, we have issues. Not just teensy-tiny issues; we have huge character flaws! God is merciful and He will not allow us to remain the selfish people that we have always been. If you belong to Him, He will discipline and train you (Heb. 12) to become conformed into the image of His Son (Rom. 8:29).

One of the primary means by which God works out the selfishness and carnality in our lives is by creating customized little button pushers, who are strategically designed to bring out the worst in us. They intuitively know how to rub us the wrong way. If you have ever wondered how on earth your children can be so effective in driving you crazy, it's because they were custom made for that purpose. Annoying you is their full-time job.

What If I Can't Stand to Be Around My Kids?

If you can come to grips with the fact that your children are, by nature, sinners, it may very well change the way you approach parenting. I remember coming home from work one day to find my frazzled wife at her wits' end. Our two-year-old had stretched her to her limit. "He is SO disobedient!" she lamented.

"Did you expect something different?" I asked. "Of course, he is disobedient. He is two years old. Our job is to train him how to become something other than who he is. He doesn't know how to do anything different unless we teach him. That teaching process is a marathon, not a sprint. It's not going to happen in one day, or one month, or even one year. We're in this for the long haul."

She breathed a long sigh and admitted, "I'm not sure that I'm up for this!" Again, I reassured her. "Of course, we're up to this! God wouldn't have given us this child if He didn't know that we were up to the challenge." You see, God is doing the same thing to us that we are trying to do with our children. He is teaching us that life is not about us. The quicker we learn this lesson, the sooner we can start passing it on to our children. You can only give to someone else what you possess yourself.

That is why Deuteronomy 6:6 says, "These words that I command you today shall be on your heart." That is the starting point.

God turns the hearts of the fathers first to the children, and only then does He turn the children's hearts to the fathers (Mal. 4:6). God wants the hearts of the parents, and He knows that if you are sub-contracting your children off to outside agencies to spare you the effort of the 24/7/365 parenting process, you are missing out on perhaps the primary means that God has established for your sanctification.

Does Homeschooling Mean I Must Give Up on "Me Time"?

I recently heard a homeschooling mother lament the fact that she had much more time for Bible reading and prayer before she had children. I can certainly relate to that feeling! It seems like the more children you have, the more the pressures and responsibilities of life crowd out the things that we consider luxuries, such as taking naps, exercising, having a social life, or developing our spiritual disciplines. It might seem that unmarried people (or at least people without children) have a much greater chance of being truly spiritual, since they are not distracted by the hectic pace of life brought on by child-rearing. The reality is, however, that all that external pressure we experience as we homeschool our children is the means God is using to sanctify and conform us into His image. It is the anvil of everyday life (the laundry, the meals, the bills, teaching academics, etc.) that God uses to hammer us into a tool fit for His purpose.

While homeschooling certainly doesn't mean that you won't ever have time away for yourself, it does involve self-sacrifice. But that isn't a bad thing.

> Then Jesus told his disciples, "If anyone would come after me, let him deny himself and take up his cross and follow me. For whoever would save his life will lose it, but whoever loses his life for my sake will find it. For what will it profit a man if he gains the whole world and forfeits his soul? Or what shall a man give in return for his soul?" (Matt. 16:24–26).

Aren't our children's souls more important than our own personal comfort? Once God has fully captured your heart and will, He then turns His focus to your children, and uses you as an agent of His grace in their lives. Your parenting will be far more effective when you can teach your children, by your own example (rather than your mere words), how God is conquering your sinful nature and self-absorbed worldview. Yes, your children need to be homeschooled so they can be trained in the way they should go, but you need it more. When a student is fully trained, he will become like his teacher (Luke 6:40).

What If My Child Isn't Like Me in Terms of Personality?

Trying to teach a child who isn't like you is, well, trying. Of course, if you are strong-willed, teaching a strong-willed child who is like you can be a challenge as well. The fact is, it's hard to do relationships with other people, even when you are responsible for their birth.

I'm a flaming extrovert. Some of my children are introverts. My wife is quiet and gentle. Some of our children are loud and energetic. God is not taken by surprise at the differences in our family. He isn't wringing His hands, fearing that He made a mistake. He didn't give you the wrong child. He gave you exactly the right child that He knew you needed to complete the good work He has begun in you (Phil. 1:6). Be willing to be flexible and use a teaching approach that works for your child, even if it might not be the one to which you relate best. If it helps your child to learn better, go with it.

How Do You Get Your Kids to Listen to You Well Enough to Teach Them?

Homeschooling is parenting with academics. I talk a lot about the parenting and relational side of this equation in my other parenting books (see *Pitchin' a Fit: Overcoming Angry & Stressed-Out Parenting* for a very in-depth treatise on this topic). To gain primary influence in your children's lives, you need to spend more time with them than anyone else, and affirm them more than anyone else.

Homeschooling gives you the context to be able to do both. It will be what you make of it. Some parents homeschool their children, but they don't adequately focus on the relational aspect. If your children lose respect for you, then you can't teach them anything. Again, the goal of homeschooling is not so much to cram information into their heads. It is to help them to learn how to learn and how to think, and for you to maintain proper influence, so you can continue to guide and direct them as they grow older.

Homeschooling Is Part of God's Plan to Reach Your Heart

Allow the pressures of being with your children all day, their bad attitudes and laziness, etc., to drive you to your knees. When you feel completely at the end of yourself, that's a great place to be. That is where God wants you. Then you know that you must rely completely on Him and His grace. At the end of yourself is where you will find Christ and His perfect faithfulness. It's not all about us; it's all about Him. It's not about what we do, but rather what He does in and through us.

CHAPTER 12

What Does Dad Do in Homeschooling?

I once read a secular study in which children were asked what they thought was the most important academic subject. It turned out that their answers reflected whatever subject involved the help of their father. The reason given was that children assume, since Dad is busy, if he is going to take time out of his schedule to help with one subject, THAT must be the most important one.

What this indicates to me is the power of a father's influence. Most of us men work jobs. We are busy. However, we can make a tremendous impact on our children if we are strategic in passing on what is most important.

What's a Dad to Do?

There are two duties that the Bible seems to lay nearly exclusively at the feet of fathers.

1. Training and instruction of children (Prov. 4:1; Eph. 6:4)
2. Discipline (Deut. 8:5; Prov. 13:1, 24, 15:5; Heb. 12)

For about six years, I served as a volunteer chaplain for a county juvenile center here in Michigan. Of the several hundred incarcerated young men that I have interviewed, only one or two said that they had a good relationship with their father. The overwhelming majority had NO connection with, nor had even met, their biological fathers.

From what I've observed, most young men who have positive input from their fathers simply don't end up being a menace to society and getting arrested.

The fault of our nation's moral decay can be placed, to a great extent, at the feet of fathers who have not lovingly and mercifully led their children in the ways of the Lord.

My Approach

In my home, I take initiative to make sure that I am leading family worship daily (or as frequently as possible) and that I am staying abreast of my children's spiritual, academic, and emotional progress. I make sure that I have "conversations that count" with each of them, drawing them out and probing them with age-appropriate questions to see if they have assimilated what they have been taught and are developing biblically informed convictions from the information they have received.

I seek to understand my children's personalities, natural skills, learning styles, and spiritual condition so I can lead them in emotionally, spiritually, and academically customized training and discipleship.

While some married couples may choose to handle things differently than my wife and I have, as a homeschooling father, I am usually the one taking the lead in selecting the curriculum that our children use. Part of that is that I am more plugged in to what is available or new on the market than my wife (because of my job), but it is also because I really feel that I need to take responsibility as the father to research and know what curriculum approach will work best with each child at each age level. I don't want to just dump that on my wife. I believe it is my job to at least be an equal partner in overseeing the general academic scope and sequence of my children's education.

For us, the curriculum is a means to help us lead our children to know, love, and serve Jesus. The academic subjects are tools in our hands to help them understand the world God created, and know how to use and harness its principles and laws to serve others in the name of Christ. We use work, academic studies, chores, vacation, recreation, and entertainment; it all serves together to help us fulfill our mandate as Christian parents.

If this sounds like it might take a lot of time and effort . . . it does. That's the point! Deuteronomy 6 is a 24/7 year-round endeavor. It's *supposed* to take a lot of time. Where do you find the time? Cut out all the worthless stuff you are doing that doesn't include your wife and children. For me, that means no golf game, no sports, no fishing, no watching TV after work, no newspaper, etc. If that sounds like legalism, it isn't. It's just realizing I only have a certain number of hours in each day and a certain amount of years with my children before they are gone.

The Eternal Perspective

When I stand before God, He will hold ME accountable for the spiritual training of my children. I can't hide behind my wife and say, as Adam tried, "This woman You gave me . . . *she* didn't know what she was doing!" No, I am responsible. The buck stops with me. I am thankful that my wife is a wonderful helpmeet and that she implements well the spiritual blueprints I am providing for our family, but her role is to come alongside and support the vision that I have received from the Lord and His Word. It's time for us men to grow up and take responsibility for our own families. There is absolutely no valid excuse to do otherwise.

Exhort, Encourage, and Charge

> For you know how, like a father with his children, we exhorted each one of you and encouraged you and charged you to walk in a manner worthy of God, who calls you into his own kingdom and glory (1 Thess. 2:11–12).

I read this verse one day and it really stood out to me. The Apostle Paul is speaking to the church in Thessalonica, but he gives a description of the role of a good father. It is assumed or presupposed that a faithful father will be doing the following three things with his children.

Exhorting

The Greek word for "exhorted" is *parakeleo*, which means to "call near," "invite," "implore," "entreat," or "pray." This word is used most often in the New Testament when someone is beseeching or seeking someone else to follow them or join them. There is almost a desperate cry that is implied in some cases, as someone realizes the importance of having another join them in their journey or struggle.

This is certainly the posture of a father as he says, "Now therefore, my son, obey my voice as I command you" (Gen. 27:8), or "Hear, my son, and be wise, and direct your heart in the way" (Prov. 23:19), or "My son, give me your heart, and let your eyes observe my ways" (Prov. 23:26). A good father is imploring his children to follow him as he follows Christ. This father has a vision. He knows where he is going, and he provides an invitation for his children to join him on the mission.

When I think of this word, Deuteronomy 6 and 11 come to my mind. A father leads his children when they rise in the morning, as they walk by the way during the day, and when they lie down at night.

Encouraging

The Greek work for "encouraging" is *paramutheomai*, which means to "relate near," "comfort," and "console." Not only does the father call and invite his children to come to him and follow him, but he draws them in and holds them close. He comforts them and calms their fears. He provides a safe place for them. They know that they are loved and accepted by their father. They understand that nothing can harm them when they are in his arms. They delight in the safety and security that he provides. This is not the picture of the stern and aloof father, emotionally distancing himself from his children, but rather an intimate picture of a father drawing near to his children, being a shelter for them from the ravages of the cruel world.

Charging

The Greek word for "charged" is *mastigoo*, which means literally, or figuratively, "to flog" or "scourge." The main usage for this word in the New Testament is to warn someone sternly. It is essential to note the order of the usage of this word in the verse. The idea of discipline or correction or rebuke comes *only* after the ideas of exhorting and comforting have been well-established. A child cannot properly receive the discipline of a father who has not laid the right foundation of drawing a child near and being a safe shelter. There is a need for a father to provide rules, guidelines, and boundaries for his children, but this must always be done in the context of a loving and caring relationship. As author Josh McDowell puts it, "Rules without relationship breeds rejection."[1]

Hebrews 12:7 assumes that it is the father's role to discipline his children. The Scripture is clear that a child left to himself will end up in trouble. "The rod and reproof give wisdom: but a child left to himself brings shame to his mother" (Prov. 29:15). There are many examples of fathers whose sons were wayward because of their lack of leadership: Aaron, Eli, Samuel, David, Solomon, etc. A father must not merely be his child's buddy. He must provide gentle and strong leadership.

Our Heavenly Father is our model in all of these areas. He demonstrates each of these traits in His relationship with us. Many fathers have not had good examples or models of this kind of balanced fatherhood. Some fathers do not provide any leadership or vision for their children. Some are not affectionate and affirming. Some will not provide discipline or are too harsh or abusive in their application of discipline. This makes it hard for men to lead in areas in which they themselves have not been led.

We all need to start somewhere, and if you haven't been led by a good role model in these areas, ask God to help you become the man you need to be so that *your* children will have an example to follow.

The living, the living, he thanks you, as I do this day; the father makes known to the children your faithfulness (Isa. 38:19).

Endnotes
1. Josh McDowell, "Helping Your Kids to Say No," *Focus on the Family*, October 16, 1987.

CHAPTER 13

Can Every Family Homeschool?

One wonderful benefit of homeschooling is that it can be as flexible and diverse as the families represented. We are not all the same. Some homeschoolers are rural, some urban, some suburban. Every ethnicity is represented.

The early modern-day homeschooling movement was dominated by Caucasians, most of whom were unschoolers or fundamentalist Christians. Today, homeschooling is embraced by people of every conceivable background.

Ethnically Diverse Homeschooling

Dr. Brian Ray, of the National Home Education Research Institute (NHERI), conducted research on black homeschoolers in 2015 and found, "Black homeschool children's high achievement test scores were very remarkable. Parents without teaching certificates helping their children from a traditionally low-achieving minority group should cause all educators and social advocacy groups to take special note."[1]

According to the National Center for Education Statistics, in 2011: "Among children who were homeschooled, a higher percentage were White (83 percent) than Black (5 percent), Hispanic (7 percent), and Asian or Pacific Islander (2 percent)."[2] Every year, resources become more expansive and more affordable.

Information and support is plenteous. In the years to come, we can expect to see the number of minority families choosing to home educate continue to increase.

Working Parents

According to researcher, Dr. Lawrence M. Rudner:

> The overwhelming majority of home schooling parents are married couples (97.3%), compared to only 72% of families with school-age children nationwide. Furthermore, 76.9% of home school mothers do not work for pay, while 86.3% of those who do work, only work part-time. Nationwide, in 1996, only 30% of married women with children under 18 did not participate in the labor force.[3]

I know of scenarios where a mother is the primary, or full-time, income maker for the family, and the father stays home and teaches the children. This sometimes includes scenarios in which a father faces an illness or physical disability, the wife has greater earning potential, the father simply desires to do the teaching, etc.

There are even situations I've observed in which both parents are employed. They have arranged their schedules so that one parent is always home with the children, or there are only short gaps when one parent must be gone (child care is provided by trusted friends or relatives for those short periods). While a father working nights and a mother working days (for example) is surely not an ideal long-term scenario (it puts a lot of strain on the family unit), families have done it successfully in the short-term.

Single Parents

Some single parents have found ways to start their own businesses or work from home (as my mother did in the 1980s). This enables them to be at home with their children and still earn an income. In cases in which a single parent must work outside the home, and private Christian schools are not affordable or available, often grandparents are willing to help provide oversight and direction for the child when the parent is away.

With the advent of online schooling and video instruction, grandparents (or any trusted and responsible adult) can be present to make sure the child is staying on task with their studies during the day. It is obviously more difficult for single parents to homeschool, but there are thousands of single parents who have proven they can successfully home educate their children. I am living proof of this because of what my mother did.

Grandparent Homeschooling

Besides parents, grandparents are the only people group who have a special commandment from God to teach children. "And that you may tell in the hearing of your son and of your grandson how I have dealt harshly with the Egyptians and what signs I have done among them, that you may know that I am the LORD" (Exod. 10:2).

In today's world, grandparents sometimes end up raising, or at least partially raising, their grandchildren. Whether you are a part-time influence, or a full-time caregiver to your grandchildren, the impact you may have is immeasurable. I would point all grandparents, whether they are homeschooling full-time, or simply seeking to be a support and encouragement to their children, to visit www. GrandparentsOfHomeschoolers.org.

Foster/Adoptive Families

Many states do not permit parents to legally home educate children who are in foster care. Many adoptive families, however, have chosen homeschooling. When an adopted child enters your home (assuming the child is not a baby), they will have many adjustments. Adopted children often suffer with attachment issues. They need love and acceptance and personalized attention, not distance and institutional approaches to education.

Parents at home can understand the strengths and weaknesses of each child, and tailor the education to fit unique needs.

You may want to take a period of six to nine months and forego as much of the formal academic training as you possibly can. The last thing you want during an introductory season is to have relational stress between you and the child because you are trying to push them further than they are willing, or capable, of going. I would encourage, at least initially, an educational approach that is highly relationship based, rather than formal and structured. Find fun field trips to do together and lots of hands-on opportunities that make learning interesting and enjoyable. Find some age-appropriate books to read aloud together. It will encourage relational bonding and may open up discussions. Find a local, or online, support group of families who are also homeschooling adopted children, so you can ask questions and learn from those who have shared experiences.

Military Families

Military families face many unique challenges because of deployments and frequent relocations. It is often difficult for them to find support on base (if they live in military housing), and their lifestyle often precludes them from plugging into regular support group or co-op activities. Because of the long separations during deployments, the scenario is also very similar, in many cases, to the single-parent families.

In addition to these struggles, they often have a hard time being part of a regular church. Military chapel services often lack the depth of discipleship or specialized classes that families would expect to find in a local church. Fathers who are away from their families can still keep in touch and help with homework through email or video conferencing. It takes more effort and intentionality, but you can still be connected even when you are away.

Increasingly, there are online social media groups, expressly created for military homeschoolers, that can provide an encouraging community of people who have shared experiences. These groups are certainly not a replacement for local relationships, but they can help to give you insights from other parents who have been where you are now. When you move into a new state or country, always remember to check with HSLDA.org to ensure that you have all your legal bases covered for your new location.

Missionary Families

If God has called you into full-time missions, you have a wonderful opportunity to demonstrate to your children that the Kingdom of God is much larger than they may have imagined. You should remember, however, that your family is your first mission field.

The history of missions in the 20th century is, in many ways, a sad one. The prevailing thought among most mission boards was that missionaries should send their children away to overseas boarding schools, so that they could focus on the work of evangelism. This was so misguided and anti-scriptural. Missionary kids (MKs) soon gained a reputation for being rebellious and for rejecting the Christian faith.

Thankfully, much has changed, and most mission boards now understand the importance of parents keeping their children with them on the mission field and giving them a Christian education within a family context. I recently heard of one missionary family, serving in the Middle East, who wanted their children to be in school, so they enrolled them in a Muslim school. The irony seems so obvious to me. They had traveled across the world to teach the Muslims to be Christian, but they sent their Christian children to school so they could learn to be Muslims. Surely the Lord desires for our children to serve alongside us, even on the mission field. The testimony of a godly family is powerful in any language or cultural context.

International Families

Homeschooling is growing across the entire world. I have personally been blessed to speak at homeschooling conferences in Japan, Russia, Mexico, and several Canadian provinces. Parents everywhere love their children and want what is best for them. Homeschooling laws vary in every country, from lenient to completely forbidding home education altogether.

In 2016, a group of international homeschooling and human rights leaders signed a manifesto of sorts called "The Rio Principles" at a conference hosted in Rio De Janeiro in Brazil. It included this bold declaration:

> The right to home education is the fundamental right of families, children, and parents clearly derived from all the above-mentioned rights and implied by them, especially by the freedom of thought, conscience, and religion, cultural rights and parental rights. Therefore, the duty of the states to respect and ensure this right is a necessary part of their obligations according to universal human rights standards.

States shall:

- explicitly recognize in their internal legislation the right of all parents to freely choose home education for their children;

- respect and protect the freedom of the parents to choose the pedagogical approach in home education;

- not interfere in home education except in cases of a serious violation of a child's rights that caused substantial harm and which have been justly proven after due process of law;

- prevent any discrimination with regard to access to the higher education and employment on the ground of education choice, including choice of home education;

- protect the freedom to engage in home education at any time without undue burden on the child or the parents.[4]

There is a growing groundswell of interest and support for home education from every continent. With the expansion of distance learning options, the translation of learning resources into non-English languages and a growing legal and legislating advance in global homeschooling freedoms, we can only expect to see homeschooling once again become a worldwide phenomenon.

Road Schooling

Being involved in itinerant speaking ministry, much of my life is spent on the road. To maintain family unity, I try to take either one child (to spend one-on-one time) or for longer trips, I endeavor to bring my entire family. Our longest road trip so far has been 66 days away from home. We drove a 15-passenger van and a 12-foot cargo trailer. We divided our time between staying in homes and motels. We do a lot of crock-pot meals, fast food, and hospitality dinners in churches and homes. It's not for the faint of heart, but it is part of the work that God has called me to do.

During such a travel season, it is very difficult to do formal book learning. As a substitute, we try to find learning experiences on the way. On one trip, we visited Mt. Rushmore, Yellowstone, Rocky Mountain National Park, and Grand Teton National Park. On another one, we visited the Grand Canyon and Meteor Crater in Arizona, as well as a fire engine museum, musical instrument museum, and much more. We even went horseback riding!

Our children gain so much life experience during these trips that cannot be gained from merely reading a book. It also gives them a point of reference so that when they read about geographic locations or historic events, they remember being there and learning about days gone by. The wonderful thing about homeschooling is being able to think outside the box. Learning is not relegated to reading textbooks. It should be integrated into all of life. Deuteronomy 6:7 tells us that we should teach our children as we "walk by the way." In today's world, that includes as we "drive by the way." We should take our children with us whenever we can and teach them as we do life.

Endnotes

1. Dr. Brian D. Ray, Ph.D., "African-American homeschool parents' motivations for homeschooling and their Black children's academic achievement," *Journal of School Choice* (2015), 9:71–96.

2. J. Redford, D. Battle, and S. Bielick (2016), *Homeschooling in the United States: 2012* (NCES 2016-096), National Center for Education Statistics, Institute of Education Sciences, U.S. Department of Education, Washington, DC, https://nces.ed.gov/fastfacts/display.asp?id=91.

3. "The Scholastic Achievement and Demographic Characteristics of Home School Students in 1998" by Lawrence M. Rudner, Ph.D. A copy of the full report can be found at https://www.hslda.org/docs/study/rudner1999/FullText.asp or see the peer-reviewed online journal Education Policy Analysis Archives at http://epaa.asu.edu/epaa/v7n8/.

4. http://therioprinciples.org/.

CHAPTER 14

Are You Cut Out for This?

When I was growing up, my mother did not allow us to own a video game console. Even though "state-of-the-art" entertainment had come into its own through Commodore® and Atari®, my sister and I (homeschooled as we were) had to make do with . . . wait for it . . . BOOKS!

But that doesn't mean that we never played video games. On occasion (we weren't allowed much socialization, don't you know!), we were able to visit friends or relatives and join them in a rousing game of Pac Man® or Pong®! (Am I old or what?!)

I remember that one of my friends had a rather unethical approach to his gaming. When his virtual life was threatened, just before he was annihilated by some digital fiend, he'd reach over and hit a reset button on the console. Wham! Just like that, he was back in business with a brand-new life and better circumstances.

A Day Gone Wrong

Have you ever felt like doing that in life? Some days just don't start out right. I had one of those days just last week. I awoke to see my beautiful baby daughter cooing sweetly in her crib. I smiled and picked her up, only to feel that something was not quite right. I quickly looked down, and saw that my shirt had a big brown stain right in the middle of it. This was an explosion. Neck to ankle. All the crib sheets, everything.

So, it started there and continued to unravel. For some reason, I decided to do something we hadn't done all year. I thought, "It's a beautiful day. I'll bless my wife and hang our clothes out on the clothesline. There's nothing like harnessing the power of free air and sunshine!" That went well, until it didn't. It poured bucket loads of rain shortly thereafter.

My toddler came to greet me with double nasal drip. "What's wrong with you?" I asked. Here we go. Another round of runny nose. Bummer. Then there was the child who decided to hide all of the clean laundry they were supposed to fold underneath the couch. Sigh. And wave after wave of misfortune unfolded.

What Do You Do When You Feel Done?

Unfortunately, life doesn't come with a reset button. You usually can't just crawl back under the bed sheets and start all over. There are still children who need your attention, and the daily responsibilities just keep on emerging.

So, what do you do in a situation like that? How can you help to set things back on the right track?

There is a story I love of Susanna Wesley, the mother of evangelist John and songwriter Charles. At times, living in a small house with numerous children, she would feel overwhelmed. She had no place to go to get away from the chaos. So, to have a "reset," she would take her apron and throw it over her head and take five minutes of prayer and quiet time alone with the Lord. Her children had learned not to interrupt mother when she was "taking five."

Sometimes, it's hard to find a quiet place, but the place to go in our moments of stress, or feeling overwhelmed, is to the Lord in prayer.

What about Illnesses or Chronic Fatigue?

It is especially difficult to keep going when recovering from a new birth, or when facing a physical ailment. In times when a parent (especially a mother) is bedridden, academics may need to take on an entirely new dynamic. Sometimes formal schooling needs to be completely benched for a few weeks until Mom is back on her feet. Or perhaps the focus can temporarily shift to video instruction, or for longer durations, online schooling.

While it is not always available, there is often help available from your local church, and/or homeschool support group, or co-op. People usually want to help if they know about the need. I've known of many situations where people have suffered in silence because they didn't want to be a burden on others. That seems noble, but we are commanded, as Christians, to bear one another's burdens. Let the Body of Christ minister to you when you are down. Often, people will provide freezer meals or will take your children to the park for an afternoon.

Extended family can also be a much-needed support in such circumstances. Again, sometimes that option isn't available to you, but as members of the family of Christ, we need to be willing to reach out to others. I know we are always excited to get to help and serve others in need. We don't see it as a burden, but rather as a blessing. I'm sure there are people in your life who would feel the same way. The main thing is to continue being the parent, as much as possible, even if you must do so from a bed or recliner. Someone else may be able to clean the floors and dish out dinner, but only you can be the parent. This is also a good reason to teach your older children how to do chores and how to cook (assuming they are old enough). They can really be a benefit to you during tough times.

Where Does Our Help Come From?

The Psalmist surely felt overwhelmed when he prayed:

> From the end of the earth I call to you when my heart is faint. Lead me to the rock that is higher than I (Ps. 61:2).

> I lift up my eyes to the hills. From where does my help come? My help comes from the LORD, who made heaven and earth (Ps. 121:1–2).

While our circumstance may not change, we can certainly recalibrate our internal spiritual compass by turning our focus to our "True North," the Lord of heaven and earth. Prayer may not immediately change what is happening around us, but it certainly can change us! When we remember that God is still in control, and that He is allowing these circumstances to mature us and help us grow, then we will not give over to fear, despair, and hopelessness. We can stand firm and know that God is allowing this testing for His glory, our ultimate good, and the eventual good of others. We are being conformed into the image of Christ through our difficulties.

> For which cause we faint not; but though our outward man perish, yet the inward man is renewed day by day. For our light affliction, which is but for a moment, worketh for us a far more exceeding and eternal weight of glory; while we look not at the things which are seen, but at the things which are not seen: for the things which are seen are temporal; but the things which are not seen are eternal (2 Cor. 4:16–18; KJV).

A New Leaf

I love this poem called "A New Leaf" by Kathleen Wheeler:

> He came to my desk with a quivering lip,
>   the lesson was done.
> "Have you a new sheet for me, dear teacher?
>   I've spoiled this one."
> I took his sheet, all soiled and blotted
> And gave him a new one all unspotted.
> And into his tired heart I cried,
> "Do better now, my child."
> I went to the throne with a trembling heart,
>   the day was done.
> "Have you a new day for me, dear Master?
>   I've spoiled this one."
> He took my day, all soiled and blotted
> And gave me a new one all unspotted.
> And into my tired heart he cried,
> "Do better now, my child."[1]

New Mercies

In the midst of one of the strongest laments in the Bible, we find these incredible words of hope and cheer:

> My soul is bereft of peace; I have forgotten what happiness is; so I say, "My endurance has perished; so has my hope from the LORD." Remember my affliction and my wanderings, the wormwood and the gall! My soul continually remembers it and is bowed down within me. But this I call to mind, and therefore I have hope: The steadfast love of the LORD never ceases; his mercies never come to an end; they are new every morning; great is your faithfulness. "The LORD is my portion," says my soul, "therefore I will hope in him." The LORD is good to those who wait for him, to the soul who seeks him. It is good that one should wait quietly for the salvation of the LORD (Lam. 3:17–26).

Isn't it amazing that right smack-dab in the middle of our pain and suffering and difficulty is a promise that God will show us new mercies with the rising of each new sun? We truly do get a "reset button." God's grace enables us to start over. That's the story of redemption: new beginnings. All of this is possible through Jesus, who conquered death and the grave. His resurrection power now lives in us through the Holy Spirit. We are not alone. We have an abiding comforter who will never leave us nor forsake us, even until the end of the world (see Heb. 13:5).

Do you need a restart today? Cry out to God, and ask for His divine help and intervention. He may not make all the bad things disappear, but He will remind you of His presence and power to be with you in the midst of your storm.

Endnotes

1. "A New Leaf," by Kathleen Wheeler. James G. Lawson, compiler, *The Best Loved Religious Poems* (Grand Rapids: Fleming H. Revell, 1961).

CHAPTER 15

Won't I Be Wasting
My Own Education?

Some parents are concerned about staying home to teach their own children because they feel they will be wasting the money they spent on their own higher education.

Reportedly, only 7 percent of the U.S. population is represented by a single-income home with two parents and children, in which only the husband works outside the home.[1] Although there are exceptions, most homeschoolers tend to fit into this demographic. In this sense, they are a bit of a throw-back to a more traditional America that was lost shortly after the "Leave it to Beaver" era died. Today, it is assumed in our culture that both parents will work.

In fact, when arguing for a mandatory military combat draft for women, some feminist legislators like Hillary Clinton (who supported the concept) argued that the success of the career woman has already proven that children can survive just fine without parents in the home to raise them. The thought that both parents would be removed from the child's life is not a shocking concept to those who have already essentially embraced it as a normal way of life.

Latchkey Kids

Do children fare as well when they are deprived of at least one full-time parent?

For more than three million American children between the ages of 6 and 13, the experience of coming home from school to Mom and apple pie is only a dream. These children end — and often even begin — their school day in houses with no adult supervision. Armed with only the key to the front door, such so-called "latchkey" kids (plus an estimated 50,000 preschoolers) fend for themselves while their parents are occupied in the workplace.[2]

What are the effects of this situation on the well-being of the child?

The effects of being a latchkey child differ with age. Loneliness, boredom and fear are most common for those younger than 10 years of age. In the early teens, there is a greater susceptibility to peer pressure, such as alcohol abuse, drug abuse, sexual promiscuity and smoking, adaptation to difficult situations. Socioeconomic status and length of time left alone can bring forth other negative effects. In one study, middle school students left home alone for more than three hours a day reported higher levels of behavioral problems, higher rates of depression and lower levels of self-esteem than other students.[3]

Parents make the claim that they are working two jobs and putting their children in public school because it is best for the children. In reality, however, the children are left trying to cope with a scenario that is relatively unique to our age, at least when you consider 6,000 years of previous human history.

The number one reason children are put into this position of essentially being raised by the government, media, and nannies is because parents have been told that they should pursue "the American Dream," and that they need both incomes and that this is ultimately best for the child, even if it doesn't appear so. Who it is ultimately best for is the corporations and the government bureaucrats who profit from the labor of the worker. The government lures both parents into the workforce so they can pay taxes. A portion of those taxes are given to government-sponsored child-care workers and educators who essentially raise the children, *en loco parentis* (in place of the parents). The additional tax revenue goes to make the government bureaucrats wealthy.

Even a child can see the fallacy of this logic:

"Mommy, why do you have to go to work?"

"I have to go to work so I can pay for people to watch you during the day."

Children know they are getting the short end of this deal. Why can't parents see it as well?

Making More Money

There are two ways to increase your net earnings:

1. Earn more.
2. Spend less.

I would contend that the "earn more" theory, as it relates to households with children is, in many cases, a bad approach to "getting ahead." The expense involved of having both parents work, combined with the emotional and relational cost of being separated from your child, usually does not put the family further ahead when all things are considered equally.

The Hidden Cost of Two Incomes

Allan C. Carlson, professor of history at Hillsdale College, has argued that the actual take-home pay from the second income is not very significant, especially when you calculate the money spent to keep Mom out of the home. "The income gained from a second working parent is often spent on day care, second cars, and restaurant bills."[4]

According to the National Center for Policy Analysis, in 1960 very few mothers worked outside the home, but today, two-income families actually have less combined income (after taxes), lower savings percentage, and far more credit card debt than families who lived on one income a generation ago.[5]

After factoring child care, work clothing, transportation and meals, taxes, and extra social activities associated with work-related relationships, experts suggest: "If both parents in a household earn the median income, how much of the second earner's income is a net gain? After deducting for childcare, clothing, a car, meals, and tax benefits, that $51,017 goes down to around $24,000 — less than half the actual earnings."[6]

Another hidden cost of two incomes is the physical and emotional drain that working outside the home puts on the wife/mother. While many women attempt to keep all the plates spinning, and do an admirable job, their attention is divided, and they often have very little left at the end of the day to invest in the relationships that mean the most to them. This often takes a toll on marriage relationships as well as the children. I know of a couple with no children in the home, who made the decision to have the wife work from home, because it was too taxing on their marriage trying to coordinate both schedules. They didn't have time to just be together. With children, it is much more difficult.

Wasting Your College Education?

I don't mean to sound cruel here, but the fact is, statistically, you are probably already wasting your college education, even if you never have children.

According to a study published by the *Washington Post*: "In 2010, only 62 percent of U.S. college graduates had a job that required a college degree. Second, the authors estimated that just 27 percent of college grads had a job that was closely related to their major."[7]

In today's economy, getting your degree to pay for itself is increasingly difficult. I think people need to carefully consider whether higher education is such a vital need at all. As a home-schooled graduate, I intentionally chose not to attend college. I knew what I wanted to do with my life, and I knew that I didn't need a college degree to achieve my goals. I was a relatively educated person and didn't need a piece of paper from a university to validate me or boost my ego or self-image. My wife took some distance education college classes but discontinued them when we were engaged. Neither of us have regretted our decision to forego obtaining a degree. The only thing we missed out on was a lot of expense and several years of our life spent in pursuit of a degree we wouldn't use. When we got married, we had no debt, and besides a modest mortgage that was well within our means, we have never had any kind of debt at all (even with nine children currently living in our home). Being debt-free enables you to have flexibility to make the best decisions for your family (which, for us, includes homeschooling our children). While I'm not advocating what my wife and I did as a template for all families, I can tell you that I prefer our choice over the dozens of stressed-out, overworked, tired, emotionally drained 30-somethings I know who are both working and trying to pay off their exorbitant college debt.

Wasting Your Life?

To know if you are wasting your life, you first need to understand what your life's calling and purpose is. What does God want you to do with your life? God gives us each special gifts, talents, and opportunities. You may have trained to be a classical pianist, or an engineer, or a lawyer, or a chemist. You may have spent years of your life and tens of thousands of dollars (or hundreds of thousands of dollars) preparing for a career in a particular field.

This issue is particularly relevant for women, as about nine out of ten stay-at-home parent situations reflect the mother staying home while the husband works. In some cases, the income from the mother may be more than the husband, in which case some couples decide to swap roles. The father stays home and does the homeschooling while the mother works. I know several families who have done this. It often works well for the children, although, in my observation, it usually puts more strain on the marriage in the long run.

If you are considering the major time and investment you have made thus far for your career, and weighing it up against the decision to homeschool your children, my suggestion is to remove "sunk cost" from the equation. It will help dramatically in clearing up your decision-making process.

Sunk Cost

Economists refer to the phenomenon of "sunk cost" when they discuss investments. Suppose you purchase a $300,000 house when the real estate market is bullish and, years later, the housing market crashes and it is valued at only $100,000. What should you do? At that moment you must decide, "Do I believe the price of this house will go back up, or do I believe it will stay the same or decrease?"

If you believe the housing market may recover, you should hold on to that house and wait out the financial turbulence. But if you have reason to believe the price of the house will only go down in value, you should sell it. It if is worth $100,000 today and will be worth $75,000 by next year (with no hope of return), you would be foolish to hang on to it for one more day. The reason people do so poorly in investments, in many cases, is because they are bringing the emotional baggage of their "sunk cost" (the $300,000 they paid) into their decision. People often factor sunk cost with relationships as well. "I know my boyfriend hits me, but we've been together for three years, and I'd hate to think I've wasted three years on a dead-end relationship."

If you turn on a road and realize it is not a through road, but is, instead, a cul-de-sac, you can't say, "But I've already been driving on this road for 5 minutes! I don't want to waste all that time going back to the main road and starting over!" If the road you are on cannot take you where you want to go, you need to start over. If you burn your dinner, you can't say, "We're just going to eat this charcoal, because I spent an hour on it, and I don't want to start over."

Sunk cost is a reality of life. The question that is before you in this moment is, "What is the best thing for my child?" Period. That's it. If you are a parent, that is the factor that is on the table. You need to set sunk cost aside. Would my child benefit the most from me investing my time and energy directly in his or her life? In almost every situation, that answer will be "Yes!" Children need their parents. They need time (quantity and quality) with their mom and dad. You will almost never regret time that you allocate to invest in the life of your child.

I've heard many guilt-ridden parents at the end of their life who lament the fact that they were too busy and didn't spend enough time with their children. But I've never heard one parent say, "I just regret that I spent so much time with my children and I wish I would have given more time to the office (or the factory, or whatever)." Your child is something you can take into eternity with you. Your job is not. Your career is not. Your degree is not. Your money, cars, house, and yard will not go to heaven with you. Only humans have eternal souls. The rest will all fade away, be forgotten, and be essentially meaningless in a hundred years. Why not invest in eternity?

Endnotes

1. http://www.prb.org/Publications/Articles/2003/ TraditionalFamiliesAccountforOnly7PercentofUSHouseholds.aspx.
2. http://article.sciencepublishinggroup.com/ html/10.11648.j.ajns.20150404.19.html.
3. Ibid.
4. Allan Carlson, "Rediscovering the Family," *National Review*, January 26, 2004.
5. "Is the Two-Income Family Worth It?" February 11, 2004, http://www. ncpa.org/sub/dpd/index.php?Article_ID=3938.
6. Erica Rawes, "The Not-So Obvious Costs of a Two-Income Household," May 21, 2014, https://www.cheatsheet.com/personal-finance/the-not-so-obvious-costs-of-a-two-income-household.html.
7. https://www.washingtonpost.com/news/wonk/wp/2013/05/20/only-27-percent-of-college-grads-have-a-job-related-to-their-major.

CHAPTER 16

What about Public
School at Home?

Imagine a two-lane road. On one end is a large government monopoly that seeks to control every facet of education and eliminate all competition. People who have their children in this system, and many who work for it, are usually oblivious to the perils of such a monstrosity. Or they see the dangers, but they don't know how to get out.

On the other end of this highway is complete educational freedom. This is what I like to refer to as "parent-directed, privately funded, family-centric, home-based education." In this model, parents, not the government, decide what approach is best for their family. One lane leads to control and limited options, the other to unfettered choice.

Along this road are various rest areas. For families who are leaving the brick-and-mortar government school, the first stop may be virtual public (or charter) schools.

Public School at Home

Mary is a single-parent mother, living in the Detroit Public School system. She has two sons, ages 14 and 11. They are constantly being offered drugs, enticed by gangs, and exposed to a terrible social atmosphere, not to mention deplorable school facilities and failing academics.

Mary decides the best path for her boys is to get them out of the harmful social environment of the brick and mortar school, and enroll them in a public school at home program. While she must work to provide for the family, her mother, who lives in an apartment off their house, is available to be home with the boys during the day. Mary decides that with the accountability from the school system, and physical oversight from her mother, this would enable her boys to at least be home, away from much of the peer pressure. They will be in an environment where she is more aware of what they are being taught during the day.

This model is not considered by law to be official homeschooling, even though the academics are being learned in the home. This is still public schooling. However, it is a better form of public schooling. You still can't use a religious curriculum, and you are still under the state's requirements and regulations, but at least your children will be home in a physical sense.

Public School and Homeschooling Hybrids

Another stop along the road is called "Public School / Homeschool Partnerships." In this model, you are considered to be, in most cases, a private home educator. Many partnerships require that a student take at least two online classes and two seated classes through the local public school district in order to qualify. In exchange, the partnership student can receive some extra benefits like swimming lessons, band practice, basket weaving, or horseback riding.

When a family signs up with a partnership in Michigan (one state where this approach is being implemented), there is no additional regulation to them, other than reporting to the local school district (which is not required for non-partnership homeschooling families in the state). Many, or possibly most, Michigan families choose not to inform the government of the fact that they are home educating. They do not want to attract unnecessary involvement from a truancy officer or local school authorities. The local school district, in most cases, in exchange for giving out a few small benefits, gets as much as 85 percent of the total annual tax funding for that school year. So even in areas where student funding is as low as $10,000 per year, per student, the local school district receives at least $8,500 in tax funding for each of these homeschooling students who enroll.

If I were a school administrator looking to increase my revenues, I'd trade occasional basket-weaving classes for $8,500 all day long! That's pretty good money for a non-core class or two (all partnership classes must be non-core elective studies)!

At this point, many families cannot see any reason not to participate in these programs, and granted, there do seem to be some benefits. Parents get a few activities or classes for which they personally do not have to pay out of pocket.

Considerations

The problems that I see with partnership programs are as follows.

Funding Government Schooling and Increased Government Spending

Personally, I want to support education that is completely free from government control. When I participate in a partnership, I am supplying my local school district with extra funds that they do not currently have. I make government bigger, not smaller, when I help local school districts qualify for more tax revenue. I also put a tremendous tax burden on my neighbors, as they must pay for the bulk of my child's "free" activities. Unless I am paying more than $8,500 a year in taxes, I am not fully paying for even one of my children to participate in these programs. That means someone else — perhaps an 80-year-old grandmother living alone in a house she owns in my neighborhood — is having to pick up the tab. If I have five children in a partnership program, the tax burden my family generates is potentially $42,500 per year. Over ten years, this could be $425,000 in additional taxes incurred on Michigan taxpayers for my children to learn basket weaving. If ten of my friends (with the same number of children — some will have more, some less) also do this, that means our little homeschool group of ten families could cost Michigan taxpayers as much as $4.25 million over ten years. That's a lot money to provide a few music or swimming lessons.

The thing is, nearly all of these classes can, and should, be taught privately, through local privately funded homeschooling support groups or co-ops. Many parents have expressed that they don't like paying a small fee for these services, or volunteering a few hours a week in exchange for free classes. I guess what comes to my mind is that if it isn't *that* important to you to invest a little of yourself in this process, is the activity itself truly all that important? Our culture has embraced an entitlement mentality, in which we believe we are owed "free" things, simply because we want them. Ultimately, nothing is free. Someone is paying for these services. If we are not fully funding them ourselves, then the money is coming from people who are being forced to pay for our child's activities against their will. It is also being redistributed by a bureaucracy that does not have your best interests in mind.

Funding Nonreligious Education

While the classes/activities in which my child is enrolled may not be deemed "religious," the extra tax revenue I generate for the local school district by having my child participate in a partnership, goes to fund many beliefs that, as a Christian, I do not want to fund. I do not want to fund the theory of Darwinian evolution being promoted as a proven scientific fact. I don't want to fund the promotion of revisionist history in the textbooks, as the Christian influence in our country is dismissed and sometimes ridiculed. I do not want to fund the promotion of situational ethics, and moral relativism. I do not want to provide additional dollars for the distribution of condoms in schools. Children are taught, with our tax dollars, that the Bible is not a fixed reference point for moral behavior, but instead, everyone can decide for himself or herself what is right or wrong. I don't want to fund transgender/LGBT propaganda, where young children are taught that sexuality is fluid, that there are no genders, and that any sexual activity between consenting adults is morally good. I prefer to defund these efforts, not contribute an extra $8,500 per year, per student, to these causes.

Social Environment

I recently talked with a mother who homeschooled her daughter until age 15. When her daughter turned 14, she enrolled her in a public-school partnership so she could take dance lessons and swimming. Her daughter quickly made friends with other students in the public school, who replaced her former friendships with teens in the private Christian co-op of which she used to be a part. The daughter requested that she attend a brick-and-mortar public school for her next school year, since all her current friends attended there. The mother agreed. They are no longer homeschooling.

This is where we see that the educational road goes in both directions. While we are thankful for the single mom in Detroit who found a better option for her sons, in this case, however, I am concerned about the fact that a family who was experiencing complete educational freedom, in a Christian atmosphere, is now in a government-controlled school where God is not allowed and where most of the students are going in the direction of the world, not of the Lord.

The Abolition of Homeschooling Support Groups

In many places where the government has competed with privately funded, Christian homeschool groups and associations, by offering similar services for "free," it has had a devastating impact on the latter. In many places, dozens of privately funded groups (co-ops, support groups, and state homeschooling associations) have either ceased to exist, or have been reduced to only a fraction of what they once were. The net result of this is that the government monopoly over education grows larger and stronger, and decentralized, parent-directed groups, who oppose government control, decrease. This eventually even eliminates the groups who do legislative and legal work to protect homeschooling freedoms in each state. Homeschooling conferences and support networks have faced a sharp decrease in participation as thousands of Christian homeschooling families have flocked to eat from the hand of the government. Government is now their provider and "support group," rather than God and their Christian brothers and sisters. It is my desire to see Christian parents choose the path of freedom, rather than dependency and control.

CHAPTER 17

What about Vouchers for Homeschoolers?

For those not familiar with the concept of school vouchers, it is the idea that instead of sending your child to a local government school that is mandated to your school district, you can receive funds from the government (in the form of vouchers) that could be used to pay tuition at a parochial, private, or home school of your choosing. The thought behind this is, "Tax money is my money, and therefore, I should be able to spend it however I like."

The whole idea of accepting school vouchers for private education is wrong-headed in many ways. Now granted, the NEA and leftist bureaucrats are against vouchers, as they see them pulling more children away from "public" schools, which they believe are essential for helping children to become good citizens. Anything that the liberal education establishment is against must be a good thing, right? Well, in this case, no.

What Is Wrong with Vouchers for Homeschooling?

It is a bad idea for homeschoolers to accept school vouchers for these reasons (and perhaps more):

1. To argue for vouchers is to imply that the government has a valid, compelling interest in the education of

children. I disagree with this premise on several levels, but for the extensive rationale behind this, you will need to read my book *Education: Does God Have an Opinion?* God has given children to parents to feed, clothe, shelter, and educate — not to the government.

2. Vouchers are confiscatory and amount to nothing less than legal plunder. (For more on the concept of "legal plunder," I refer you to Frederic Bastiat's excellent little book on government and economics entitled *The Law*.) The concept of taking from the rich (or those who have) to give to the poor (those who have not) may sound good in the Robin Hood fables, but it is nothing less than an immoral breaking of the eighth commandment of God: "Thou Shalt Not Steal." It is no less immoral simply because it is the government doing it. In fact, as the agency that is established by God to uphold righteousness, it is that much worse.

3. Once the government takes your money, it is no longer "your money," it is now "their money." It is now in their possession to spend as they see fit. Imagine that you were robbed at gunpoint by a thug in a back alley. Suppose that he told you that he would give some of the money back if you bought a car with it. He would dictate what percentage you would get back to spend on the car and which dealer to buy it from. You could pick from any car on the lot (because he is *so* generous). Then, of course, he would own the car and drive it, but you could ride around with him. What a kind and generous offer! At least it would be a way for you to get *some* benefit out of "your" money. Would you lobby Congress, asking them to give him the right to do this? I hope not, but that is what you are doing if you promote school vouchers.

4. Whoever pays for an education controls it. There is no such thing as a free lunch when the government is involved. Look at states where children can receive a "free" home education through government charter schools. (All charter schools are government schools, by the way.) By law, parents are not permitted to give their children a religious education in a government-controlled home learning program, because it would be considered an "establishment of religion" for the government to pay for sectarian religious instruction. While the government paying for religious education may seem like a good thing to you, imagine how you might feel (as a Christian parent) if your tax dollars were being giving through vouchers to a local Islamic Jihadist school in your neighborhood. Would you really want your hard-earned dollar taken from you (with the threat of losing your property if you don't pay your property/school tax) to fund a religious system that would be teaching young children that Jews and Christians are infidels? For vouchers to be fair, you couldn't discriminate against religions that you don't agree with. That is a major reason why the government shouldn't be in the education business, because all education is inherently religious in nature. If you receive government funds, you can be certain you are ultimately going to give up freedom of choice.

Alternative Options

Far better than taking money from the government in terms of voucher handouts (complete with strings and regulations), it is best to insist that government keeps their hands out of our pockets in the first place. How can this be done? Well, you could do away with compulsory education entirely (which I would support, by the way), but this will never happen in my lifetime. So, the next best thing may be creating tax deductions for those who opt to educate their children through private or home schools. Exempting homeschoolers from the school portion of their property tax would be a great start!

Another option is the nongovernment-funded Coverdale Education Savings Accounts (ESAs). This would allow individuals or businesses to put money in their own private savings account, earmarked for educational purposes. These work like Health Savings Accounts (HSAs) or Individual Retirement Accounts (IRAs). In this case, you get a tax deduction for the money you put into the account, but it is your money, not the government's, so they should not be able to tell you how to spend it. As of the writing of this book, these savings accounts are only available for you to spend for public school use, but if legislation could be written to allow public and private schools to use them, Christians would have to ensure that there were no strings attached as to what kind of curriculum you could use.

In Minnesota, you can deduct the amount you spend on educational supplies as a homeschooler on your taxes, but you must state that it was not for religious materials. That tends to be the catch. No religious instruction when the government is involved.

Some advocates for school reform have advocated for tax credits for homeschoolers. They feel this allows homeschoolers to get back a bit of the money they are forced to spend on a system they don't use. The difficulty with many of these plans is equality. What about couples who have never had children? What about retired people who are no longer utilizing the system? Once you start opting some people out of taxation, where do you draw the line?

Educational Socialism

Most people today, even most Christians, have been so immersed into the worldview of educational socialism, they see absolutely nothing wrong with it. In fact, most Christians will fight tooth-and-nail to defend such a system. They will promote the idea of the "common good" and talk about "social contract" and such. In the end, they are very committed to the notion that the free market is simply inadequate, as a system, to provide adequate education for all. They believe that, ultimately, only socialistic methods are sufficient, and we must have a socialist "safety net" to catch students who would otherwise fall through the cracks.

Even self-proclaimed Christian conservatives, who would never think of voting for a Democratic political candidate, are saturated in a socialist ideology (forced redistribution of wealth is essential and necessary) when it comes to education. It is my contention that Christians need to have their thinking radically reformed on this matter. We need to learn to base our thinking on Scripture, not on our own experiences or on cultural norms and expectations.

It was for this reason that I wrote my book *Education: Does God Have an Opinion? (A Biblical Apologetic for Christian Education and Homeschooling)*. As noted, it outlines what education should look like if we approach it from a scriptural standpoint. It is my contention that the Bible is authoritative in every area to which it speaks, and it speaks extensively to the topic of education. I implore you to get a copy of the book, read it, and share it with friends. It is, in my opinion, the most important and comprehensive book on education from a biblical worldview that you could buy.

Conclusion

So, what is the solution? For now, the best thing is for parents to pay for their own children's private Christian education, knowing full well that they are being robbed by the government who makes them, at the same time, also pay for the education of all the children in their neighborhood through the public schools. This is the option that my wife and I have chosen, and I am hoping that many other freedom-loving parents across America and the world will choose the same option. Only when education is completely privately funded can it be free from tyranny. Only when education is free from compulsion and tyranny can it truly be called "education."

CHAPTER 18

How Can You Teach Multiple Grades?

(By my wife, Brook Wayne)

Often, when people think of homeschooling more than one child, they picture teaching each child every single subject, in a formal classroom setting. They then begin with the next child and repeat the process in his specific grade level. This approach would leave even the most dedicated mom dizzy and stressed! Homeschooling families have found ways to creatively teach outside the box of the formal, grade-specific, classroom model, and not only succeed, but flourish. Here are some strategies families teaching several grades at once implement.

Family-Integrated Learning

One of the biggest benefits for homeschooling families is being able to grow, learn, and relate as a family. Given the fact that we are all born with a sinful nature, the proximity that homeschooling provides gives all of us (including parents) plenty of opportunities for repentance and forgiveness. However, the closeness of this setting is a huge benefit for our child's development as well. Families with several children can really benefit from utilizing family-integrated learning as part of their home education by teaching many subjects all together. This works particularly well for apologetics, history, literature, and science.

Instead of teaching multiple grades in each subject, the academic model can be simplified by having your children all learn together. This creates bonding by sharing experiences. A synergy happens as older ones can pass on their understanding of the material, and larger discussions ensue. Assignments can be tailored for younger students, while older students may take on additional and more difficult options. For example, in history, this might look like basing your current study in one book or textbook, read aloud together and discussed together. It may include a video or movie that portrays the era of study, enjoyed by the entire family. Perhaps the youngest will create a re-enactment of what they are learning. The upper elementary students can give a short speech, complete with drawings, and the high schoolers can present a more advanced essay or speech. The cohesiveness of this strategy has given our family a lot of advantages.

Our current homeschool year includes a 1st grader up to a 12th grader. Integrated teaching is difficult when you are focused on teaching the three "R's," which usually requires one-on-one teaching. Even so, we have a group of four that are close enough in ability that we teach writing, spelling, and apologetics in a group setting. This variation brings a lot of simplicity to our home.

One-on-One Instruction

Giving personalized instruction is especially imperative during the very youngest academic years. The payoff of diligence here is rewarded down the road when a capable, self-directed student has been produced. So, don't ever feel the repetitive nature of your individualized time is a waste. Begin with a solid foundation in phonics, then reading, the very simplest mathematics, and instruction in writing. Enthusiasm in these subjects will provide your young student with the tools for later independent learning. The beauty of this kind of teaching is that short spurts (5-minute stretches for five-year-olds, 15-minute stretches for seven-year-olds, etc.) goes a long, long way. Don't fool yourself that long, formal class instruction is needed during the early years. Your children are missing out on long hours lost standing in line, waiting for some 20 or 30 other children to assemble, sit down, and quiet down. In the homeschool setting, you can get right down to learning. Snatch moments here and there, and set the books aside when important character issues come up (and they will . . . frequently!).

To not miss out on the uniqueness of individual needs, I set up an "interview" time each year. I sit down with each of my children and ask questions about their favorite color, which subject they find the most difficult, something they want to learn or do in the coming year, their favorite dinner, favorite subject, etc. This helps me focus on the area my child himself thinks is the hardest, which areas he thinks he excels in, and gives me ideas to help to bend his education toward his particular tastes and interests.

Special Needs and Toddlers

Children with learning challenges will need more individualized attention to meet their personalized needs. In these cases, I would still encourage including this child in the family-integrated stud-ies. Assign projects and tasks that fit in with this student's interest and ability, but much more of this student's work will need to be customized due to necessity. Perhaps it will need to be more audi-tory. Perhaps more hands-on projects or flashcards are needed. The strain for many families in this type of situation is time. Unlike some of your other students, your learning-challenged child may not readily get to the point of independent study. I feel that parents need to maintain a perspective as they work on academics with a special needs child, to keep relationship first. Keep the conversations going. You may be tired of going over basic things day in and day out, but when you just enjoy being together, it won't be so stressful. Once healthy routines and pat-terns are established, start having siblings participate as a "study buddy." They need to see your gentle heart of encouragement, as a parent, but then siblings can come alongside and help serve.

The Buddy System

Recruiting your older children to help teach their younger siblings can have some very positive effects. The process of teaching someone a skill or passing on information requires the teacher to stretch in their communication skills and patience, while challenging them to see the world through new eyes and overcome obstacles. It is good for older children to learn to serve the younger. A word of caution: It is the parents' responsibility to raise and teach their own children. Discretion and moderation need to be used in utilizing the time and talents of your older children.

What about Toddlers?

Toddlers (and babies!) can add so much excitement and adventure to your home! We've had one or two in our home continuously for the last 18 years, so I'm not quite sure what homeschooling looks like without the lively interruptions of young fry. Life with tiny people is never going to run entirely smoothly, so learning to work around their needs is a must. Planned mini-breaks can go such a long way in helping the little ones stay cheerful while you educate your older children. This might look like reading a little board book together or serving a snack, bringing out a special toy or holding a child while you teach a math lesson to an older sibling. Toddlers have a special desire to run the household, and will do so if allowed! Keeping them directed with toys, coloring, books, and other little activities can help them grow into a routine themselves, which prepares them to be attentive students for you down the road.

Individual Assignments

Children mature at such different rates that the time a youngster can be ready for following through a study assignment on his or her own can vary widely. Once a child can read and do simple math computations, begin "testing" your student by assigning a subject or two to do on his own. This can be as early as second grade for some, but is generally a little later. Don't freak out if your child doesn't do well. Some children are not ready, mature enough, or capable of this until somewhere in the middle school years! A truly educated young person is someone who knows how to learn. That doesn't always come naturally for children, and this is where they need you.

The most basic skills, such as reading and basic math, are the tools needed for a child to begin learning on his or her own. Once those are in place, teaching takes on much more of a guidance flavor that directs students in which materials and books to cover, and draws on the young person's own discoveries and thinking skills.

Several years ago, as our family read through the *Little House on the Prairie* series, I was intrigued with the descriptions given during Laura's teaching years in a one-room schoolhouse. She had multiple grades to teach, and her experiences sparked my interest in how the long-ago one-room schoolmarms handled the diversity of their students' needs. One of the examples that stuck out to me was that the students were required to read through their lesson before going to school. It was essentially their homework. This can work beautifully for the homeschooling family as well, strengthening each child's ability to learn on their own, and maximizing Mom's actual teaching time. Plus, it doesn't hurt a child to have that review time built right into his day.

These independent study sessions should start out very short, say 15 minutes. As your children grow and spend more and more time accomplishing their academic studies on their own, regular and consistent accountability is a must. Setting an appointment in your day/week will go a long way into making sure no academic holes are left hanging.

Yes, You Can Homeschool Multiple Grades

Sometimes, homeschooling moms with more than one child can be made to feel inadequate because they aren't giving six direct hours of teaching to each student. The fact is, moms and dads are uniquely qualified to care deeply about their child's academic and spiritual success. They care enough to do whatever it takes to nurture their child in the struggling moments, and rejoice with their child when in his or her victories. My husband always tells me that parenting is not a sprint. It's a marathon. Our children's education won't happen in a day. It is built on lesson after lesson. Some of those lessons won't go as planned, many will be interrupted, some won't take. But in the course of 18 years (give or take), the facts you pass on, the truth you instill, the patterns you establish, and conversations you initiate, will all produce a harvest that will be well worth the effort!

CHAPTER 19

What about Special Needs Education?

The entire structure of institutional schooling supports the concept of average. Students who do not fit the median are often shoved aside or left behind. Even terms like "standardized testing" reveal that the goal is to create a "standard" or "average" performance from each student.

The problem is, no child is truly average. Each child is unique, special, and diverse in the way he or she thinks and learns. Nowhere is this more clearly evidenced than with students who have more pronounced differences, like learning difficulties or special aptitudes. Gifted students and special needs students alike (the margins of the student body) are usually neglected or funneled into special classes designed to focus on their unique needs and challenges.

In most cases, home education works so much better than institutionalized schooling, even for students who face difficulties. No one knows your child as well as you do, and no one could care as much.

Follow the Money

The federal government has created programs like IDEA (the Individuals with Disabilities Education Act) to provide extra funding for students who are diagnosed with a learning challenge. From a pragmatic viewpoint, there is both a positive and negative outcome associated with this. The positive is that students have extra funding to provide specialized attention that they otherwise would never receive. The negative result (besides an immense extra tax burden for citizens) is that local school districts are often very aggressive in diagnosing and labeling students with learning "disabilities," because they can often double their annual funding, per child, if they can tap into the federal money pipeline.

As an aside, this is not meant to be a criticism of the many wonderful special education teachers who honestly seek to help students. The system and those who work in the system need to be distinguished.

ADD/ADHD

A perfect example of a money-motivating diagnosis is the exponential tsunami of students (mostly boys) who have been labeled with ADD or ADHD since the 1980s. Some authors have called this "the war against boys." Many students, who would have simply been called spirited, or even normal, in the 1950s, are now deemed mentally ill (the original term for ADD was "minimal brain dysfunction"). Millions of students have been medicated in government schools, many of whom are simply boys who aren't wired to sit behind a school desk for seven hours a day.

I was a hyperactive student myself as a boy. It was exceedingly difficult for me in a classroom setting to focus on academic studies. I was far too enthralled with everything going on in the classroom. The flexibility and customization of a home learning environment worked far better for me. I could do academics for 15 minutes and then go run around outside for 5 minutes. Or I could hang upside down off the couch and read my book. Or I could sit in my room with the curtains drawn and take a test, so I wouldn't be distracted by what was going on outside. Homeschooling worked far better for me than classroom learning. I would encourage you to read my book *Full-Time Parenting* for a chapter I wrote on "Helping the Hyperactive Child."

Dyslexia/Dysgraphia

When I was homeschooled, it became evident that I had some struggles with dyslexia. I learned to read several hundred sight words pictographically. That means that when I looked at the word "tree" I memorized it as a picture and would say the word in the same way that I learned to say the word when I saw a picture of an actual tree. Because I developed a large list of many sight words, it took a long time for others to catch on to the fact that I didn't possess the ability to decode and sound out unfamiliar or difficult words phonetically. Even two years in private Christian schools (in second grade and sixth grade) did not reveal my struggle.

The only reason that I eventually overcame my reading struggles was because I was homeschooled. Had I been placed in a "special class" in school, I would have resisted to the point of refusing to learn. I needed remedial help, but I was too proud (at 11 years old) to allow other students to see that I couldn't read. I ended up having to go through phonics once again, and relearn, from the ground up, what I faked and cheated my way through when I was younger. Because it was only my family (who cared about my success and whom I trusted) involved in the process, I submitted to it (as painful as it was).

While dyslexia has to do with reading struggles, dysgraphia is a writing disorder. The Learning Disabilities Association of America describes it this way:

> A person with this specific learning disability may have problems including illegible handwriting, inconsistent spacing, poor spatial planning on paper, poor spelling, and difficulty composing writing as well as thinking and writing at the same time.[1]

Whether your child has difficulties with reading or writing (or both), you can, as a parent, connect them to good resources without sending them to government schools.

I highly recommend the writings of Samuel Blumenfeld on the topic of literacy and reading disorders. While not a Christian organization, you can get helpful information on the topic of dyslexia from the International Dyslexia Association: www.dyslexiaida.org.

Vision / Auditory Disorders / Speech Therapy

I highly recommend that all parents have their child's eyes and hearing checked. So many learning struggles, and perceived learning "disorders," stem from students simply not being able to see or hear properly. One of our sons had a very difficult time following through with instructions. I took him to a local private, Christian college that has a speech/pathology department. They do diagnostic hearing tests. His hearing tested fine in terms of volume and frequency, but I knew there was still an issue, so I pressed for more extensive testing. He was diagnosed with having Auditory Processing Disorder. This is a condition in which the child can hear the actual sounds, but everything gets jumbled up in the brain, and he or she gets confused.

With this understanding, we could adjust the way we instructed him. We sought to eliminate excessive background room noise (sometimes by going into a quiet room) and gave him personal instructions without other distractions. This worked much better for him. He could have been labeled as ADD because he didn't seem to be paying attention when we spoke to him, but more precisely, it was a hearing/brain issue that just needed a special approach.

Our son also needed speech therapy, which we obtained from the same school. The blessing of working with the local Christian college is that the students needed practice with real children. Therefore, the school gave us incredibly low rates for his therapy. We paid only $20 an hour (split into two half-hour sessions, of $10 each) a week! Since we were self-pay, this worked great for us. A local doctor had quoted us a $5,000 package, because he was hoping to bill it to insurance. We ended up having the same treatment (probably better actually) for only about $1,000. While I understand this is a lot of money on one level, we would not even consider putting him into a government school in exchange for something we could provide for him through other means.

Autism

There are entire websites and books that have been written on the topic of homeschooling students on the autism spectrum (including Asperger's Syndrome). I won't try to replicate that information here. I will say, however, if you have a child who deals with auditory, visual, spatial, tactile, or other sensory disorders, they need a customized educational approach, not a one-size-fits-all institution. Homeschooling gives your child the ability to dial in on their unique learning methods. I've met autistic students who will sit and read the encyclopedia for hours, or create endless multiplication charts. That works fine in a homeschooling environment, but not well at all in a classroom full of distractions.

Gifted Students

Here is a description of a "gifted" student from the National Association for Gifted Children:

> What is Giftedness? Children are gifted when their ability is significantly above the norm for their age. Giftedness may manifest in one or more domains such as: intellectual, creative, artistic, leadership, or in a specific academic field such as language arts, mathematics, or science. It is important to note that not all gifted children look or act alike. Giftedness exists in every demographic group and personality type. It is important that adults look hard to discover potential and support gifted children as they reach for their personal best.[2]

Homeschooling is ideal for the gifted student because it allows her or him to work at their own pace. They don't have to be held back by the "bell curve" of the classroom. Rather than being sequestered away in an elite boarding school, they can have all the advantages of private schooling at home. They can have a customized curriculum, and even tutors, in person or online, all from the relational context of being home with the family.

Resources

One of the longest-lasting Christian organizations dedicated to helping homeschooled students with special needs is the National Challenged Homeschoolers Associated Network (NATHHAN). Their website is NATHHAN.com. They have a large collection of articles on many specialized topics on their Christian Homes and Special Kids website (CHASK.org).

HSLDA.org has an extensive resource site for students with special needs covering the "four learning gates" of:

- Visual processing
- Visual/motor (writing) processing
- Auditory processing
- Focus/attention processing

And topics such as:

- ADD/ADHD
- Apraxia (see Speech Disorders)
- Autism (Asperger's and PDD)
- Auditory Processing Dysfunction
- A Struggling Right Brain Learner
- Dysgraphia (writing problems — penmanship and composition)
- Dyslexia
- Gifted Children
- Intellectual Disabilities
- Sensory Processing Dysfunction
- Speech Disorders
- Transitioning to Post-Secondary
- Vision Impaired

Under each category, they have an extensive list of books, articles, and websites that contain specific information for each of these resources. I highly recommend becoming a member of HSLDA and utilizing their free and member resources.

Other Physical and or Mental Limitations

One of the wonderful benefits of being a homeschooling parent is that you get to learn right along with your student. Nothing reflects the heart of life-long learning more than putting yourself back "in school" so to speak, to learn the things that you do not know (or have forgotten). When you have a child who has special needs, you need to become a student of your student. You need to read, study, and become an expert on your child. It is certainly wise to utilize outside resources (books, videos, seminars, experts, coaches, tutors, mentors, therapists, etc.), but in the end, you are still the parent.

The more involved you are in the process of your child's training and development, the better. The goal is to share our lives with our children and to help bear their struggles and burdens. Sure, it would be easier to just dump them off and let them be someone else's responsibility. But God didn't give that child to someone else. He gave that child to you. He loves your child and you. You may not be big enough for this task, but He certainly is. He has not abandoned you to do this alone. He will be with you. He can do in and through you what you cannot do on your own. As you seek God, He will direct and lead you to teach, train, and love your special needs child.

> If any of you lacks wisdom, let him ask God, who gives generously to all without reproach, and it will be given him (James 1:5).

Endnotes
1. https://ldaamerica.org/types-of-learning-disabilities/dysgraphia.
2. From the NAGC.org homepage.

CHAPTER 20

What about Extracurricular Activities?

M any parents fear that their children will miss out on extra-curricular activities if they homeschool. What about sports, band, graduation, prom, homecoming, clubs, drama, debate team, etc.?

If sports or social events are keeping you from teaching your children at home, I would encourage you to ask yourself some questions. Who is pushing the issue of these extra-curricular activities? Is your child pushing you because he or she wants to participate? If so, what are the motives? Are their motives wise or frivolous? Are they pushing for these activities because they want to free themselves from parental influence? If so, why? Are there deeper issues that need to be discussed?

Could it be that you, as a parent, are trying to relive your high school years vicariously through your child? Fathers often think fondly of their teen years playing football, or mothers nostalgically reminisce about their teen proms. They want their children to have these same experiences. Does your child really desire these activities, or are you imposing your feelings on your child?

Are you considering these activities because you are being pressured by others outside of your family (grandparents, neighbors, friends, etc.)? Could it be that you are simply trying to fulfill societal expectation?

I would suggest that children and teenagers are not wise enough to make major decisions about their future. They need parents to help guide them through these difficult choices. I would also suggest that it is not wise for parents to impose their own personal ideals and experiences on children who may end up being quite different from them. Very few homeschooled children will have a sense of loss regarding something they have never experienced.

NFL Career?

One lady told me she felt God wanted her son to play professional football, so she quit homeschooling him and sent him to a government school. She said he wouldn't have a chance of going pro unless he played on a high school team.

I don't know whether it was God's will or not. As far as I know, he hasn't been signed yet, but at least his family had a goal. Most parents know God hasn't called their children to be professional athletes; they simply feel that the social interaction would be good for them. I would question the necessity of such extracurricular activities, but if a parent feels they are essential, often the benefits of physical exercise, team cooperation, competition, and social activity can be met through community, church, or even homeschooling sports leagues.

There is even a national homeschooling basketball tournament! My point is, if you simply feel a need to have them involved in social activities or get physical exercise, you can do that without sending them to the government schools.

Some see sports as a ticket to financial scholarships for their students. If your child wants to play sports, you should evaluate the call of God on the child's life and pray for direction. Does God really want to use your child in the sports arena? Help your child to realistically evaluate his or her skills and potential.

When I was ten, I was convinced I would be a professional baseball player. After a year of little league, I realized that baseball wasn't my gift. I simply wasn't good enough. Unfortunately, some parents won't encourage their children to honestly face their ability (or lack of ability). I can just imagine how much time I might have wasted going to school, thinking I was going to be a big leaguer when, in fact, God had totally different plans for my life.

Today, homeschoolers can often play on private or government school sports teams without attending the school. You would need to check the laws in your state to see what is available where you live. Personally, if I knew that our local government school district was going to be receiving additional tax revenue for including my child, or if there were additional regulations regarding our homeschool (what we could teach, standardized testing, etc.), I would not choose this route. But this is a legal option in many states.

Competitive sports are often organized and led by unbelievers who sometimes encourage overly aggressive and violent behavior. My little league baseball coach taught us to win at any cost. He told pitchers to deliberately hit batters with high batting averages. He showed us how to take out a second baseman (for the year) to break up a double play. He told me once when I didn't plow into the catcher, "If he gets hurt, that's his problem!" I know there are many coaches who would be appalled by the actions of my coach, but it does happen. Every game we lost, we learned a whole new list of vocabulary words, so perhaps it had some merit on the educational side!

Another consideration is the attitudes and actions of non-Christian players both on the field and in the locker rooms. We are told in 1 Timothy 4:8: "(F)or while bodily training is of some value, godliness is of value in every way, as it holds promise for the present life and also for the life to come." What is our priority? Are we willing to put our child in a situation in which they may be enticed to compromise morally, simply to obtain what we are clearly told is of a lesser value?

Recreating the Government School?

Some years ago, I was talking with the director of a special program that offered co-op classes to homeschoolers. The organization he led owned a very large building that was essentially a very large school building but for homeschoolers. It had lockers, a library, classrooms, and a basketball/multi-purpose sports facility. Homeschoolers from across the city utilized this building and offered programs and options that weren't easily facilitated by individual families.

The director told me that he was so discouraged by what he was seeing that he was planning on resigning his job. He told me that parents would drop their children off in the morning and pick them up in the afternoon. They would simply rotate from one "co-op" class to another for eight hours a day. In some of these "homeschooling" families, both parents worked full-time. It was essentially an almost free private school for their child.

He revealed that a recent sweep through the school lockers had revealed drugs, alcohol, and pornography that was in the possession of underage "homeschooling" students. I couldn't help but think that the "schooling" had overshadowed the "home" in these so-called "homeschooling" families.

I remember also hearing about a homeschooled teenaged girl who got pregnant at her homeschool prom. We've truly come full-circle in many ways in terms of trying to replicate the government school system for our children.

But should they be our standard? Should we even want our children to experience those things?

What about Co-ops and Support Groups?

For many years, Christian parents banded together to provide extra-curricular, non-elective programs through support groups and co-ops. These groups were parent-controlled and parent-directed. Some classes or sports were led by paid tutors or coaches, but parents were usually personally involved through volunteering and funding the activities.

Over time, the government school system has sought to compete with these privately funded groups by actively recruiting homeschooling students to take many of these courses or offerings through the local school district. As I described in the chapter on "Public School at Home," the schools receive partial or full annual funding for each student they attract. Because they get thousands of dollars per year, per student, for offering a couple of non-core, elective classes, they have a great profit motive in enticing privately funded homeschoolers.

Increasingly, these private Christian support groups have decreased in number, so much so that in many places where many groups once thrived, there are none remaining. That means that the government school has become the center of social activity for many homeschooling families, and the worldly influence of non-Christian students and facilitators has often undermined what parents say they want to promote in the home: a biblical worldview undergirding the student's instruction.

The main reason for turning to the government for these programs has usually been cost, and sometimes the fact that parents don't need to participate. He who finances the education controls it, and Christian homeschooling is all about relationship. So, at least in my mind, we are moving further away from our objectives, rather than toward them, when we opt for non-Christian influence in exchange for money.

Christian support groups can provide much-needed encouragement for moms, and not merely activities for the children. As much as online social media groups are convenient (and quickly becoming a replacement for in-person support), we need to have relationships with people we know in real life. There is much value in watching veteran homeschooling families interact with their children. You can learn what to do (and sometimes what not to do) by watching and observing genuine families in a real-life setting.

One thing to avoid, however, is the competition that can sometimes occur, especially in co-ops. Quite often there is a desire for us to push our children beyond what they can do to keep up with the mega-moms at the co-op. This will only leave you feeling discouraged and defeated. Support groups and co-ops can be great resources if kept in their place. They are tools to help you to teach your own children more effectively. When they have begun to replace you and your influence, reconsider their use.

When they begin to burden and weigh you down with stress and feelings of inferiority, perhaps you need to do something else.

Too Much Activity?

Honestly, for most American families (even those who home-school!), I believe we have too much booked into our schedule. Parents feel their children will "miss out" if they aren't involved in soccer, band, theater, art, swimming, horseback riding, etc. You can only do so much before you end up getting exhausted and neglecting truly important things. Learning how to say no to over-activities is important. While homeschooling support groups or co-ops can provide field trips and enrichment classes, you should ask how much of what you have scheduled is truly vital. You can never truly be successful in life, or in homeschooling, until you learn how to say no to lesser options. Remember, the good can be the enemy of the best. Choose only the best and most productive paths for your children. You can't do everything. Pick the best things. "Test everything; hold fast what is good" (1 Thess. 5:21).

CHAPTER 21

What about High School?

One of the greatest concerns homeschooling parents have is teaching advanced academic subjects. Many of us did not do well in certain subjects in high school, and we barely remember the material (if at all). Teaching chemistry, algebra, or calculus is a daunting task, especially if you did not excel in these subjects, or major in them in college.

How Do I Teach Advanced Subjects?

When I entered my freshman year of homeschool high school, I had a very distinct "disadvantage." I was not a good student. I had made great strides in overcoming my dyslexia and ADHD, but reading was still difficult for me. I read almost no books that were not required reading until after I finished high school. At that time, my mother was a single parent, who was running a publishing business she founded and homeschooling my four younger sisters (ages 8, 6, 5, and 4).

I found academics to be dry, boring, and, for the most part, not very applicable to the real world. Why did I need to read Shakespeare, do algebra, or study other subjects that I would likely never use in my occupation or other endeavors in life? I wanted to be done! I told my mother that I wanted to drop out of homeschooling and just get a job.

Can you imagine that? Being a homeschool dropout?! How great would that look on a resume? Wisely, my mother presented me with the accelerated distance-learning plan I talked about earlier. Remember, she told me that if I applied myself, I could finish four years of high school in just two! Yeah. That's what I thought! No way! I'd die from the strain. She wrote up a lesson plan and showed me just how much I'd have to do each day and week to make it work.

It turned out that I could finish my 12th-grade studies just one week before I turned 16. She then promised me, that if I wanted to, I could get a job. After serious deliberation, I decided that was my wisest course. I did four years of Abeka video school in two years! And, no, I didn't have a social life! The blessing of this approach was that it enabled me to have in-class video instruction, just as I would have in a Christian school classroom. (They literally video-recorded live classes, and I would sit and watch them, just like I was in class, and then I read the textbooks and took my tests.)

My mother told me that it was not her job to hold my hand through high school. She had essentially dropped out of high school in 9th grade, so she did not know any of these advanced subjects or how to teach them. She also had four little girls who needed her focused attention. She provided the curriculum (which was not cheap!), wrote the lesson plans, provided accountability to make sure that I stayed on course, graded my tests, and turned me loose to be a self-directed learner.

She reminded me that it was not her job to teach me everything that could be known in life. Rather, she had taught me how to read, how to think (how to reason), and how to study. Now it was time for me to teach myself. I had an opportunity to learn. What I made of it was up to me.

I believe I received a very adequate academic education. I am very thankful for the sacrifices my mother made to ensure that I could learn at home, without the distractions of high school and all the drama connected with that scene.

Which Subjects Are Truly Important?

Every state has different legal requirements regarding which subjects must be studied in high school. When I was being homeschooled, homeschooling was illegal where we lived, so we obviously weren't very concerned about meeting the state's requirements! My mother wisely decided that certain subjects were simply not that important for me to study. She had me study Algebra 1, even though I vehemently protested, because she knew that it was going to be important if I ever decided to take the college route someday. It also is a good practice for developing problem-solving and critical thinking skills. I did not go to college and have never used algebra in my life, but it didn't kill me to study it. It almost killed me, but it didn't completely kill me!

She later changed her views on this and did not require my younger sisters to study algebra at all. A couple of them ended up taking college classes after high school and struggled tremendously with algebra, since they had no experience with it. It is very difficult to be a parent. Your children may complain if you heap too much on them academically, but they may also complain later if they don't feel you pushed them hard enough! It's hard to win sometimes.

In my case, my mother made me take basic chemistry, but not calculus, trigonometry, or advanced chemistry. I'm super thankful for her wisdom in cutting these from my workload. I have never used these subjects in my line of work, and frankly, I have no interest in learning them. She told me that if I ever needed to know them later in life, I could go back and study them on my own time. I have never felt the need.

I believe it is important to try to anticipate what interests and inclinations your teenagers have, so you can steer and direct them to the subjects that will most readily equip them for life.

What about Recordkeeping and Transcripts?

For many reasons, keeping high school transcripts of your student's studies is a very important step. Many colleges lean heavily on transcripts, and not having your paperwork can result in a lack of opportunities for your student. There are several organizations that can walk you through this process, including HSLDA.org.

Accredited Diploma

States vary on their requirements for high school diplomas. Many states allow parents to produce their own diplomas, based on parent-produced student transcripts or records. Some of these states also have legislation that mandates acceptance of these diplomas by colleges and employers (non-discrimination clauses). Check HSLDA for the laws in your state regarding credentialed diplomas. Keep in mind that there could be an issue if your student graduates in one state and seeks employment in another which may not recognize your parent-issued diploma. This is a great reason to be a paid member of HSLDA, as they will represent you legally if you run into any issues along this line.

Some states require you to homeschool through a private academy. These cover-schools or ISPs (as they are often called) keep your student's records and will issue an accredited diploma. There are also secular and Christian distance learning programs that offer accredited diplomas after completion of the coursework.

Dual Enrollment

Many community colleges offer dual enrollment options, where high school students can take college classes for credit and get a jump-start on their college education. Especially if the student is planning to live at home during the college years, this can save students an immense amount of money over other state or private college options.

Some private colleges, like Liberty University, now offer an accredited distance learning high school program, with dual credits that can be applied to higher education courses if you choose to attend their school (on-campus or online). If you knew, for example, that you wanted to study at Liberty for your post-secondary studies, it would make sense to enroll in their high school program as a jump-start toward saving time and money in college.

Biblical Worldview

It is in the final stretch of the parenting journey that it is so important to solidify your final life lessons with your "arrows," before they launch (see Ps. 128:3–4). The Gen 2 Survey, published by Generations with Vision and NHERI.org in 2015, was the largest survey of churched millennials to date (almost 10,000 young adults). The study revealed that there were several components that were very useful in terms of helping your children to embrace the Christian faith, have a biblical worldview, live a godly lifestyle, have satisfaction in life, be involved civically, and have beliefs that were similar to Mom and Dad (and correspondingly, have a close relationship with them as adults).

The key components turned out to be: close relationship with both mother and father in the early years and the later years, church attendance in the early years and teen years, and homeschooling. These three things, done in tandem, provided a powerful force toward the outcomes that most of us, as Christian parents, desire for our children. Think of it as a three-legged stool. If you take one of those legs out, the stool falls over. But there is a fourth leg that, when added to the other three, proves to be over 122 percent more successful in producing the desired outcomes than the other three alone.

It is the component of teaching your children systematic apologetics and a biblical worldview. If you use an intentional program like Worldview Academy, Summit Ministries, The Truth Project, or a biblical worldview curriculum like Master Books, that seeks to integrate apologetics into every subject at every grade level, you are more than doubling the statistical odds that your child will remain in the Christian faith. Many teenagers abandon Christianity because they become convinced it isn't defensible. They need to know that Christianity is a most reasonable faith, and it can be defended.

Nehemiah Institute (publisher of a biblical worldview assessment tool called The PEERS Test) has demonstrated through their testing that the national composite scores of homeschoolers go up substantively each grade when a student is being home-schooled by Christian parents. So, while the freshman scores for homeschoolers are not all that impressive (indicating that home-schooled ninth graders are not very grounded in the faith when their mothers and fathers are considering sending them off to play football in the local government school), their scores go up in direct proportion to the time their parents work with them and teach them at home.

There is so much that could be said about adequate life preparation for teens, and perhaps I'll address that specifically in another book at some point, but please make worldview training a priority. If you don't know how to do that yourself, my book *Education: Does God Have an Opinion? (A Biblical Apologetic for Christian Education and Homeschooling)* describes how there is no religious neutrality in education, and how every subject can be taught from a biblical worldview.

CHAPTER 22

What about College?

This topic is one in which I am a bit out of my element. At the time of this writing, my oldest child is only 17, so the entire life-launch process is mostly theory for me rather than experience. I endeavor in my writing to stay in my own lane. I write about what the Scripture clearly teaches and about what I have personally experienced and lived.

However, this topic was greatly requested when I asked fellow homeschoolers what they'd like to hear discussed in a book like this. So, I'm going to offer my views and some suggestions based on my personal thoughts and reflections so far on the journey. I fully reserve the right to modify or change my views on this in the years that follow.

Is College Necessary?

I would first like to contend with the notion that college is an absolute for all, or even most, students. My perspective on this, undoubtedly, comes from my own personal experience as a homeschooled graduate. When I finished homeschool high school, I considered going to a state university to get a degree in marketing or communications.

My mother owned a Christian publishing company, and she began hiring graphic design, journalism, and marketing students from a local private college in our town. When I conversed with them, I was shocked to find that they knew far less than I did about those topics, and couldn't even afford their own computers or design software because of their steep tuition fees. For the cost of one semester at school, they could have bought a top-of-the-line computer, the best design software in the world, and tutorials to learn how to use it. My thought was that if they wanted on-the-job training, they could have volunteered to work for a few months for free at the local newspaper, and would have gained far more practical knowledge than they were getting at college.

The worst thing I observed was that it was almost impossible to teach them anything at work, because of the fact they thought they knew everything (since they were "majoring" in that field). It really soured me toward going to college. Did I really want to invest the time and money required for a degree simply to graduate with far more debt than actual job skills?

I decided to hit my mother up for a job. For the next 20 years, I worked as the marketing director for her company. I led a national sales team, helped publish three national magazines, handled wholesale distribution for books we published, and essentially morphed into being the business manager for the company. All of this, without a college degree. I began doing national conference speaking when I was 19, and my first book was published at 25 years of age. I have had a successful career and was blessed to begin marriage with no debt. Living with almost no debt (a reasonable mortgage is the only debt we've ever incurred) has been a massive benefit to my family. When you have little to no debt, it gives you lots of freedom and flexibility.

In my life, I have never needed, or been asked for, a college degree of any kind, or even a high school diploma or GED, for that matter. Many jobs simply do not require college degrees for employment.

Know What You Want to Do

I'm stunned by the number of students who attend college simply because it is a cultural norm (or their parents are paying their way). College is a very expensive way to try to "find yourself."

In my mind, you need to be pretty certain about your career path before you start spending thousands (or tens of thousands) of dollars on a maybe. Only 27 percent of college graduates are working in a field that is closely related to their college degree.[1] That means that almost three-quarters of all college graduates did not need their college degree to do the work they are doing today. Some occupations require a college degree, but many do not.

If you are going to be a doctor, you need to go to medical school. End of story. I don't want somebody operating on me who graduated from the online, do-it-yourself, home-study course! If you are going to cut me open, I want to see the entire alphabet behind your name! But for many other fields (especially if you start your own business), college may not be needed at all. I know I'm a bit of a maverick on this point, but Bill Gates, Steve Jobs, and Mark Zuckerberg were all college dropouts who did pretty well for themselves. Entrepreneurship is determined by the ability to think critically, understand your industry, predict changes, adjust before it's too late, and be self-motivated. None of this is specifically taught in most college settings. If you have these skills, you can succeed in life with or without a degree.

Mentoring and Apprenticeships

Personally, I am a big fan of mentoring and apprenticeship programs for homeschooled teens and graduates. Depending on the field of interest, these relationships can be far more beneficial than formal classroom study (and far less expensive). A huge part of education should be the formation of godly character. Real-life relationships that help prepare for a career are invaluable. Even for students who attend a formal college, or take college classes online, I highly recommend seeking out mentoring relationships on both a spiritual and occupational level.

Technical or Trade Schools

It makes perfect sense to me that if you want to be a diesel mechanic, a dental hygienist, an electrician, or work in HVAC, welding, hairdressing, tool and die, etc., and you need certification, you should choose a school that specializes in your field of interest. The cost is less, you finish faster, and you are more focused on classes that actually fit into your future career. Make sure you do some research to see how important the prestige factor may be for the degree your student is seeking. Will your pay be less over the long haul if you don't get a bachelor degree or higher from an actual college? In many cases the pay will be very similar if you can do the work, but do some research first.

Scholarships, ACT, and SAT

Financial benefits are extremely helpful if your student plans to attend a formal college. These are often available for academic performance based on SAT/ACT test scores. I recommend the SAT and ACT prep books by Dr. James Stobaugh (published by Master Books) as helpful study aids to prepare your high school students to excel on these evaluations. It can literally save thousands of dollars off tuition costs.

One question people often ask is regarding the academic success of homeschoolers in college. "The SAT 2014 test scores of college-bound homeschool students were higher than the national average of all college-bound seniors that same year. Some 13,549 homeschool seniors had the following mean scores: 567 in critical reading, 521 in mathematics, and 535 in writing (College Board, 2014a). The mean SAT scores for all college-bound seniors in 2014 were 497 in critical reading, 513 in mathematics, and 487 in writing (College Board, 2014b)."[2] Homeschoolers not only do extremely well in college academically, they also tend to be very socially engaged as well.

Accelerated Distance College and CLEP Tests

More and more programs are being offered through the Internet for college students. Programs like Lumerit Education (Lumerit Scholar) help guide students through a variety of online, distance learning degrees. Their program is endorsed by Dave Ramsey as an option for graduating with no debt. You can earn a bachelor degree faster for less money by saving money on dorm costs and, in many cases, textbooks. CLEP tests allow students to get credits for classes they haven't even taken, as long as they can prove (through the assessment tests) that they know the course material.

I have a homeschool graduate friend who created his own accelerated distance college approach, working mainly through Thomas Edison College for credited classes. Through intense, focused study and CLEP testing, he obtained his bachelor degree in two short years, for under $6,000! Now granted, he is more studious than most, and he didn't have a social life for two years, but it can be done.

As time goes on, this will become an increasingly desirable approach for homeschoolers who need an accredited degree. Homeschooling students are already used to studying on their own, at their own pace. Students who are highly motivated can save precious time and cost with this approach. It also saves students from the pressures of campus life and the distractions that can come along with that. While many of these classes are not Christian, it is far easier for students to navigate the coursework (or skip them through CLEP) at home, rather than in a classroom.

I also believe that in the next decade or two we are going to see a massive shift in how all education takes place. The Internet has the potential to be the great leveler in making higher education more affordable and effective. There is currently a website called ModernStates.org that claims to offer your entire freshman year of college online for free (using Advanced Placement and CLEP exams). I think we will all be amazed at how the doors will be blown wide open in the very near future as competition online becomes more robust.

Secular College Campus

Drinking: According to the National Institute on Alcohol Abuse and Alcoholism,[3] "Drinking at college has become a ritual that students often see as an integral part of their higher education experience. Many students come to college with established drinking habits, and the college environment can exacerbate the problem. According to a national survey, almost 60 percent of college students ages 18–22 drank alcohol in the past month,[4] and almost 2 out of 3 of them engaged in binge drinking during that same timeframe."[5]

Sex: 58.1 percent of all 12th graders have had sexual intercourse before finishing high school.[6] This percentage is probably much higher regarding premarital sexual activity when you consider the fact that many teenagers do not consider sexual acts other than intercourse to be "real" sex. Once students get on a college campus, away from their homes and the careful watch of Mom and Dad, the pressure to be sexually active increases exponentially.

> Kalish and Kimmel (2011) found that among 14,000 students at 19 colleges, 58% had hooked up by their senior year, with respondents averaging about seven hookups. Armstrong and colleagues (2012), studying more than 13,000 heterosexual women with a more recent version of the data set, reported that by their senior year 69% of college women had hooked up, with a median of three reported hookups, including the women who did not report hooking up. These and other studies also suggest that there has been a decline in traditional dating and courtship practices. While it is easy to interpret these findings as indicators of a culture of "no strings attached" sexuality, the activities students reported under the term "hooking up" included everything from kissing to intercourse, with intercourse being reported in less than half of all hookups.[7]

This should be reason enough for most parents to strongly reconsider secular college campuses as options for their Christian students. Then there is the worldview component.

Religion: "A recent UCLA study found many college students drift away from their religious upbringings. In the study, 52 percent of the students said they attended religious services frequently the year before entering college, but by their junior year attendance had dropped to 29 percent."[8]

According to a study by UCLA, college is becoming increasingly secular: "More (freshman) students than ever (27.5%) selected "none" as their religious preference, a 2.9 percentage point increase from 2013, and an increase of more than 12 percentage points from when the question was first asked in 1971 (Eagan et al., 2014)."[9] When "nones" (those with no religious affiliation) are combined with atheists and agnostics, non-religious students are the highest percentage they have ever been on campus.

When you consider that The Barna Institute discovered that, "less than one-half of one percent of adults in the Mosaic generation (i.e., those aged 18 to 23) have a biblical worldview,"[10] it is easy to see the almost wholesale destruction of Christian faith that K–12 government schooling and secular colleges have had on the faith of an entire generation of youth.

Incoming Freshmen Continue to Drift Left Politically

The same study showed that more students than ever now support legalized abortion (63.5 percent), homosexuality, and other leftist social causes.

> Since 1970 we have asked students to rate their political orientation on a five-point scale, from "far right" to "far left." For the past several years, greater proportions of students have identified as either "liberal" or "far left." Roughly one-third of the students (33.5%) who entered a four-year institution in the fall of 2015 identify as "liberal" or "far left," 1.8 percentage points higher than in 2014, and 3.9 points higher than in 2012. This figure represents the highest proportion of left-leaning students since 36.4% of students identified as liberal or far left in 1973.[11]

The shift from right to left politically and socially corresponds with the influence of the faculty. According to Accuracy in Academia, 8 out of 10 college professors donate money to the Democratic Party.[12] These college professors are largely socialist, progressive humanists who are highly skilled in making skeptics out of unequipped Sunday school graduates. Do not glibly assume that your child will escape becoming a statistic of moral departure. Very few Christians make it through secular colleges and universities with a biblical worldview intact.

Christian Colleges

Before sending your child to a Christian college, I implore you to read *Already Compromised* by Ken Ham and Greg Hall (Master Books). It is a frightening critique of the state of modern, Christian colleges in the United States. Unfortunately, the clear majority no longer stand firm on the authority of Scripture. Many have compromised with Darwinian evolution, humanism, and emergent theology. In fact, only 24 percent of Christian colleges teach that macro-evolution is false.[13]

Greg Hall says:

> Parents are sending their students into the schools assuming that they are going to be faith-nurturing and truth-affirming institutions. In reality, many of them discredit the Bible, and break kids down rather than build them up. That's why both of us (Greg and Ken Ham) are strong advocates for homeschooling, Christian schools and carefully selected Christian higher education, because kids are dying out there and the Church doesn't seem to care enough to do anything about it. When it comes to colleges and universities, the problem is that the majority of Christian schools seem to be just like the secular — disguised with a few Christian elements.[14]

I would encourage you to visit AnswersInGenesis.org and visit the page they have on higher education to see which schools affirm a literal view of creation and the global Flood.[15] This is certainly not the only litmus test for biblical authority, but it is an important one. Even so, I recently heard one homeschooled young lady, who attended one of those schools on the approved list, say that there were three "progressive" professors at her conservative Christian college who helped her escape her "Christian fundamentalism." She is now an atheist.

Can My Homeschooled Student Be Accepted into College?

The good news is that homeschooling is so popular now, and homeschoolers have successfully demonstrated that they can excel academically in college. Because of that, most colleges actively recruit homeschoolers. It is very rare that a homeschooled student has any difficulty gaining entrance into college. If you have a well-maintained transcript, a state-recognized diploma (HSLDA. org encourages diplomas rather than a GED in most cases), and good ACT or SAT scores, your student should have no issues at all. Being a member of HSLDA is very helpful, however, in case you do face discrimination as a homeschooler. They have successfully represented several homeschooling graduates over the years who were stone-walled by a college or university, and it was almost always quickly resolved by a letter from an HSLDA attorney to the school, informing them of the legal requirements in their state regarding homeschooling.

Trust in the Lord, Not Your Understanding

The college waters are very difficult to navigate. The goal is to seek the Lord (Prov. 3:5–6) to see what His will is for your student. Be willing to wait and be patient, even if it feels uncomfortable. If my child had no sense of life direction, before I would begin paying on a college education, I would encourage him or her to get a job or do some kind of Christian volunteer work. Sometimes people just need to take a few more years to mature and develop. That's okay. Encourage them to be active in serving the Lord and others while they sort through their future plans. Often it all comes together for them later. If it takes a while, they can start earning an income, and are at least gaining some life experience, rather than blowing tens of thousands of dollars on classes that may end up just being a waste of time for them. Sometimes, a delayed college entrance can aid in a student standing strong against the worldly ideologies due to less susceptibility to peer pressure from students several years younger.

As I said in the beginning, this is new territory for me as a parent, so I'm still praying and trusting God to lead us with our own children. I trust that God will grant you wisdom as you seek Him for direction for each of your students.

Endnotes

1. U.S. Bureau of the Census, 2010 American Community Survey, "Federal Reserve Bank of New York Staff Reports: Agglomeration and Job Matching among College Graduates" by Jaison R. Abel Richard Deitz, Staff Report No. 587, December 2012, Revised December 2014, P.8, www.newyorkfed.org/medialibrary/media/research/staff_reports/sr587.pdf.

2. Dr. Brian D. Ray, Ph.D., "Homeschool SAT Scores for 2014 Higher Than National Average," June 7, 2016, www.nheri.org/research/nheri-news.

3. https://pubs.niaaa.nih.gov/publications/CollegeFactSheet/CollegeFactSheet.pdf.

4. SAMHSA, 2014 National Survey on Drug Use and Health (NSDUH), Table 6.88B — Alcohol Use in the Past Month among Persons Aged 18 to 22, by College Enrollment Status and Demographic Characteristics: Percentages, 2013 and 2014. Available at: www.samhsa.gov/data/sites/default/files/NSDUHDetTabs2014/NSDUH-DetTabs2014.htm#tab6-88b.

5. SAMHSA, 2014 National Survey on Drug Use and Health (NSDUH), Table 6.89B — Binge Alcohol Use in the Past Month among Persons Aged 18 to 22 by College Enrollment Status and Demographic Characteristics: Percentages, 2013 and 2014. Available at: www.samhsa.gov/data/sites/default/files/NSDUH-DetTabs2014/NSDUH-DetTabs2014.htm#tab6-89b.

6. www.cdc.gov/healthyyouth/data/yrbs/pdf/2015/ss6506_updated.pdf, p. 28.

7. Martin A. Monto and Anna G. Carey (Department of Social and Behavioral Sciences, University of Portland), "A New Standard of Sexual Behavior? Are Claims Associated With the 'Hookup Culture' Supported by General Social Survey Data?" *The Journal of Sex Research*, 51(6), April 2014, p. 605–615, The Society for the Scientific Study of Sexuality.

8. "Are Students Losing Their Religion on Campus?" ABC News, Dec. 6, 2005, http://abcnews.go.com/GMA/story?id=1375842&page=1.

9. UCLA study: "The American Freshman: National Norms Fall 2015," p. 30, www.heri.ucla.edu/monographs/TheAmericanFreshman2015.pdf.

10. "Barna Survey Examines Changes in Worldview Among Christians over the Past 13 Years," Research Releases in Faith & Christianity, March 9, 2009, www.barna.com/research/barna-survey-examines-changes-in-worldview-among-christians-over-the-past-13-years.

11. Ibid, p. 31.

12. Spencer Irvine, "College Democrats as Professors," October 18, 2013, www.academia.org/college-democrats-as-professors.

13. Ken Ham & Greg Hall, *Already Compromised* (Green Forest, AR: Master Books, 2011), p. 23.

14. Ibid, p. 139.

15. http://answersingenesis.org/colleges/colleges-and-universities/.

CHAPTER 23

How Can You Find Time for Everything?

(By my wife, Brook Wayne)

Many of the organizational books on the market today guide homemakers in accomplishing household management tasks while the children are in school. The reality, for home-schooling families, is that there aren't usually long stretches of child-free time for housework. There are many hands though, and while at first it may not seem to make the work light, it definitely makes for a more integrated family that works together, plays together, and learns together.

It Requires an Entire Family Effort

It only takes one or two very little children to completely mess up a clean home. Those same little children can learn to pick up their toys and dirty laundry, and wipe up spills. Since the whole family benefits from a functioning home, the whole family should contribute to that functioning, even when their "help" isn't so very skilled.

Most young children need a lot of oversight and training to keep their chore minutes productive. During those years, Mom and Dad may need to juggle a lot of hands-on responsibility within the home. But as those little helping hands grow in maturity and skill, Mom's position changes from doing much of the work herself to one of a manager.

I like how the Berean Study Bible refers to the needs of older women to teach younger women how to be "managers of their households."

> Older women, likewise, are to be reverent in their behavior, not slanderers or addicted to much wine, but teachers of good. In this way, they can train the young women to love their husbands and children, to be self-controlled, pure, managers of their households, kind, and subject to their own husbands, so that the word of God will not be discredited (Titus 2:3–5; BSB).

A manager isn't the one who does all the work. A manager learns how to delegate and oversee. A manager trains and provides accountability.

The benefit of the whole family joining together to make the home function goes far beyond just making life easier for Mom (as beneficial as that is!). Every mom is needed in her home in the roles of nurturer, loving and supportive wife, academic teacher, guidance counselor, mentor, and spiritual advisor. Every mom will have to manage her top priorities. Simply put, if she can delegate everything and anything that someone else can do, and only do those things which only she can do, she will better be able to invest in her family.

But that whole family involvement isn't just for daily chores like laundry and dishes. This extends to showing hospitality, giving to those in need, planning and preparing for errands and trips, grocery budgeting, financial stewardship, creativity in baking, gardening, making homemade gifts, etc. It is nurtured through shared experiences, both fun times and difficult times. When the whole family must pull together, the unit is strengthened.

Life Skills and Balance

Children, though they won't always graciously express it in the moment, truly thrive by involvement with household chores.

When children are brought up with the expectation of helping to keep up the home, they are given a message that says, "I am needed here. My family depends upon me." Attached with love, that kind of message can sink deep into our children and grow a sense of satisfaction. When a child is handed meaningful chores, and applies himself to it, he will (yes, eventually!) gain life skills that will be a huge asset to him later in life. With each new skill under his belt, his confidence will grow — a confidence that will go with him later in life when new challenges present themselves.

Some believe that children should not have chores, and instead should be free to enjoy only playtime throughout childhood. There's plenty to be said for children being given time to freely explore, play games, and act out stories. Each of these expressions of playing help to fit and prepare youngsters for life as adults. In a similar fashion, you should also lead them into age-appropriate jobs, projects, hobbies, and creative pursuits. This enables them to meet the adult years with greater readiness. Furthermore, a child's play is often enjoyed and appreciated more when it is a break from normal life (rather than being the whole of their life). Work makes play taste sweet. A balance is necessary as both play and work are needed in the life of a child.

Still others believe that children should devote their time to academic improvement to the exclusion of physical tasks around the home. Much of this perspective stems from a sincere desire on the parents' part to help their child succeed academically, and thus in life. The irony is that children can benefit from physically performing chores in ways that academic pursuits can't match. Work teaches lessons like: problem solving, getting their hands dirty, being diligent in what might be considered dull activities, paying attention to detail, developing quickness and thoroughness in habits, listening for instruction, correlation between sweat equity and a desired result, and a hands-on understanding of the Second Law of Thermodynamics (the Law of Entropy teaches that everything is seeking a state of decay, and you must be constantly vigilant to ensure proper upkeep is maintained).

Relationally speaking, a child accustomed to chores from an early age will one day bring a much-appreciated dynamic to marriage.

Have a Plan

A huge percentage of Mom's stress in managing the home comes from needing to make hundreds of decisions throughout the day. Often, those decisions are about what is the most important "emergency" of the moment. What do I cook for dinner? How can I clean the bathroom with two toddlers? When do I teach my six-year-old to fold laundry when the laundry pile is higher than his head? Planning ahead won't fix every home-management ill, but it is a huge step in that direction. It helps to spend your minutes ahead of time, on paper, before you spend them in real life.

When I know that I'm making chicken noodle soup and cornbread for dinner, I can easily get out chicken to thaw the night before, prep carrots and celery, and even mix up the cornbread batter, all in spare minutes, without a lot of fuss. When I wait until 5:30 p.m. to figure out what to serve for dinner, the ensuing workload and stress is anything but streamlined. Similarly, when I know that we will have upwards of 15 loads of laundry in the coming week, I can assign my team for a grand folding party with audio books and reward them with snacks afterward.

I also pre-plan my children's chores. We've chosen to keep the assigned chores with the same person for about a year, so that he can grow in skill and speed in those areas, and so that I don't have a headache trying to figure out who is supposed to do what. Each child ages seven and up, has about four jobs a day (excluding kitchen cleanup after meals) that take about 15 minutes each. Sometimes I'll swap out one of these slots and assign a random job that isn't in our regular routine. This doesn't get the deep-cleaning done, but it helps keep the home functioning. One of the habits we're trying to put into place is to create a "family clean team" to give the house a deep clean once a week.

Clear Expectations

Frustration is bound to happen if we have general expectations that we'd like our family to pitch in and keep our homes functional, but we don't clearly designate and communicate what we expect everyone to do.

There are lots of creative and diverse ideas for transmitting Mom and Dad's desires for home tasks to their children. After some trial and error, we've found what works best for us is a checklist on which each task and requirement is carefully spelled out. This includes basic things, such as making one's bed, but then it lists approximately four tasks that are unique to each child. "Clean your room" is broken down into mini-jobs, such as pick up all toys and put away, deal with all clothing, make your bed, vacuum floor. Simply telling a child to "clean your room" usually feels too overwhelming for a youngster.

Our simple chart lists the time of day down the left side, and the day of the week at the top. This way I can specify what each child should be doing at any particular time of the day, and exactly what that entails. Free time is even scheduled in and serves as a motivation! Also on our checklist are all the study subjects assigned for the week. I can jot in as desired which pages I want a child to cover in each time slot.

Dealing with Slackers

Once you've organized how to keep the home functional, communicated those plans, and created a routine, you may still deal with a live child who does not always see the necessity of his personal involvement in chore time. Here are some ideas to help motivate your child:

1. Spend time on a regular basis talking about how your family needs every member. We all pitch in on the workload so we can all enjoy benefits like eating meals, relaxing together, taking day trips, welcoming guests, and playing together. Broaden your child's vision by

helping them see the many ways a functioning family contributes to him on a personal level, the family as a whole, and the church and community around him.

2. Nobody likes something for which they have no skill or aptitude. Spend copious amounts of time training your youngster in how to do each job, and equip him to succeed with proper tools, encouragement, and a helping hand now and then.

3. Nobody likes spending all day on chores. Show your child how long the job should take (remember, he is not up to turbo speed yet as a newbie!) and communicate that the chores you have given aren't meant to take all day. Communicate that you want him to be able to participate in a wide variety of activities. Scheduling some free time just following your chore time can do wonders in helping a child stay on task. If they know dawdling is eating into their personal free time, they will typically step on it!

Flexibility

Even with the best laid plans and an enthusiasm for tackling chores, things won't always go as planned. That's okay. Your planning isn't in vain. Sometimes it needs to be tweaked to make it more realistic. Interruptions are going to happen. Someone will come down sick. The dog will run out the front door. A child won't cooperate, or maybe you'll be blessed with a new baby. In the long run, constant application of the family schedule will make the difference and keep the family home functioning.

This Is a Season

In general, I love taking my little children grocery shopping. In fact, I rarely go shopping alone. One day recently I was in a bit of a hurry, and my three-year-old was especially talkative. She's always been like that and wants me to be very involved in every conversation. Grocery shopping for us is a bit like a massive stock up, and takes a while. My daughter was enjoying some fun banter about making pies, how fun it is to have sparkly stickers, and wondering out loud if candy bars cost two pennies each. My mind was running through my list, comparing prices, and navigating my big children pushing a separate cart.

Then I heard, "Mama, Mama! What do you think? Is it two pennies for a candy bar? I have two pennies!" I looked at my sweet daughter, so happily perched in the grocery cart, baby sister buckled in next to her, sucking on the cart handle, and I sighed. It would be so much easier to go grocery shopping by myself. It is such a big job for our family, and I could probably get through a lot faster. In that moment, however, it occurred to me that someday these little ones would grow up. Then, I thought, wow, just think how much faster these massive stock ups would be! Oh, but wait, I won't be cooking for an army then. When life gets easier down the road, I won't have the privilege of taking my little ones along with me for the ride. I will go grocery shopping, it will be simple and small, and I'm going to miss this messy, imperfect season like crazy.

Raising a family, homeschooling, and really living in our homes means there are nitty-gritty, genuine messes. There will be spilled brownie batter, stacks of books, homeschool papers, and dirty laundry. Eventually those little children will grow up and the dust will settle. It's in the very middle of this beautiful, sometimes chaotic, life that we can truly invest in our families. While you strive for keeping a functional home, don't forget to love the people who make up your family.

CHAPTER 24

Do You Know What Causes That?

Are you Amish? Catholic? Mormon? Are you a school group? Are these all yours? Are you trying to start your own baseball team? I guess you don't own a television? Do you know what causes that?

At the writing of this book, our family has nine children. In some ways, my wife and I are the poster family for homeschooling. We were both home educated. I grew up with five sisters, and she with only one brother. We both have desired to have a lot of children, and God has blessed us in that endeavor.

All the questions above have been leveled at us many times by checkout clerks at the grocery store, passersby, and even bewildered or concerned fellow church members.

There is almost a stereotype in some homeschooling circles that having a big family is a requirement. This can be a deterrent for some young couples who aren't sure that they want the stigma of being lumped in with reality TV families who have double-digit households.

Being a Large Family

We walked into a church one Resurrection Sunday morning only to be greeted with a look of utter amazement from the greeter. His jaw dropped, and his eyes were as big as saucers. "Wow! How many children do you have?!" he exclaimed.

"We have nine," I answered.

"Wow. Well, are you done?"

"Done having children? I hope not."

"Man, you guys could have your own reality TV show!"

"Umm . . . could I please have a bulletin?"

"Wow, look at them all! That's a bunch of kids! Man . . . one, two, three. . . ."

"Could we please be seated?"

"Oh, uh, sure. Hey, look at this family, guys!" (To some other ushers.) "Have you ever seen so many kids?!"

Just for the record, this was NOT a wonderful way to be received into worship. I like to think that we are a family, not a freak family. I understand that the sheer number overwhelms some people (although I do think that greeter could use some sensitivity training!). It's been many decades since larger families were the norm in society.

Living in a Small-Family Society

As of the beginning of 2016, there were 59.8 births in North America per 1,000 women aged 15–44; this was the lowest number since records have been kept since 1909.[1] To sustain population, a replacement fertility rate of about 2.1 must be maintained. In 2016, our U.S. replacement fertility rate was 1.87 births per woman.[2] We are the only nation who is growing because of immigration, rather than births.

Having a larger-than-average family in a small-family society can definitely be a challenge. It raises the question of how children will feel growing up being homeschooled. There is a sense in which, if you are born into a large family as a child, you have several cultural stigmas that you need to overcome. First, if your family is Christian, that puts you in an odd dynamic. We live in a post-Christian America, so still believing that the Bible is true, and Jesus is who He said He was, marginalizes you. In fact, less than one-half of one percent of Americans between the ages of 18 and 23 believe even the most basic tenets of a biblical worldview.[3]

So, if you are a born-again Christian with a biblical world-view, are being homeschooled (about one-half of one percent of the population), and you come from a large family, you are about as rare as a polar bear in the desert!

Will your homeschooled child grow up feeling weird and like they are a misfit in society? As a homeschooled graduate who embodies all of those dynamics, I love the fact that I don't fit in. I don't want to fit in! Average is so over-rated. We have a blessed opportunity to be unique and different, but in a good way. "Do not be conformed to this world, but be transformed by the renewal of your mind" (Rom. 12:2).

If I hadn't been homeschooled, I would not have been able to do many of the things I've done in life. So many doors have opened for me because of my unique experience of being home educated. It truly is contrast that makes something notable. Marketing guru Seth Godin once used the metaphor of a "purple cow" to describe the kind of company or product that every successful business wants to create. You don't want a bland, boring, run-of-the-mill experience. You want exceptional. People are looking for something that stands out and stands for something, in a world filled with cultural relativism and directionless living.

I am not saying that larger families are better families. I'm saying that being unusual isn't anything to run from. The goal is not to be *avant garde*, so people will think you are an oddball. The goal is to faithfully follow God wherever He leads and to face the critics and the applause with equal deference. We don't do what we do to please people. We live to please God alone.

> Whatever you do, work heartily, as for the Lord and not for men, knowing that from the Lord you will receive the inheritance as your reward. You are serving the Lord Christ (Col. 3:23–24).

Being a Small Family in the Homeschooling World

According to researcher Lawrence M. Rudner:

The distribution of children in home school families and families with children under 18 nationwide: On average, home school students are in larger families. Nationwide, most families with school-age children (79.6%) have only 1 or 2 children with a mean of about 1.9 children per family. Most home school families (62.1%) have 3 or more children with a mean of about 3.1 children per family.[4]

If you think about it, three children per household really isn't *that* big. It's not true of all homeschooling circles, but there are definitely pockets where you can find a majority of large families, and if that isn't your family dynamic, you can definitely feel out of place. Especially because children are generally held in such high regard within Christian homeschooling circles, it is possible to feel intimidated, or even looked down upon, if you don't have "enough" children. Whether the people near you actually think less of you for not having a large family, it is possible to have those insecure feelings.

This can be especially painful if you have struggled with miscarriage, health conditions, or infertility issues that have prohibited you from having more children. Just as large homeschooling families sometimes feel like social outcasts in their churches, small families often feel marginalized in their homeschooling "support" groups.

What Does the Bible Say about Children?

One of the most famous passages in Scripture that speaks to the innate value of children is found in Psalm 127:3–5:

> Behold, children are a heritage from the LORD, the fruit of the womb a reward. Like arrows in the hand of a warrior are the children of one's youth. Blessed is the man who fills his quiver with them! He shall not be put to shame when he speaks with his enemies in the gate.

It's so interesting that we don't think of children as a "reward" or a "blessing" or a "heritage" (inheritance) from the Lord in our

American culture or, frankly, even in the modern Church today. Children are seen, in many cases, as an annoyance, a nuisance, a distraction, an impediment to success, and many other negative attributes, but rarely as something to be excited about (like winning the lottery!).

Unfortunately, the anti-child worldview of Margaret Sanger and other population-control advocates has trickled down to the pews, and now most Christians think like humanists rather than biblically astute believers.

The next chapter in Psalms says:

> Blessed is everyone who fears the LORD, who walks in his ways! . . . Your wife will be like a fruitful vine within your house; your children will be like olive shoots around your table. Behold, thus shall the man be blessed who fears the LORD (Ps. 128:1–4).

In the Bible, children (and families) are always spoken of with great honor.

> Did he not make them one, with a portion of the Spirit in their union? And what was the one God seeking? Godly offspring. So, guard yourselves in your spirit, and let none of you be faithless to the wife of your youth (Mal. 2:15).

One of God's primary purposes in the creation of marriage was not merely producing offspring (which we see in God's command in Genesis 1:28 to "Be fruitful and multiply and fill the earth and subdue it"), but raising up *godly* offspring. Christian discipleship starts in the home, with our own children.

Some people believe that we live in such an unstable world that we shouldn't be having more children. They feel that the culture is too wicked, the economy too poor, and the future too unknown to risk bringing more children onto our planet. Is this God's view? I find it instructive that at one of the lowest points in the history of the nation of Israel (the Babylonian captivity), God commanded His people to have more children, not less.

> Take wives and have sons and daughters; take wives for your sons, and give your daughters in marriage, that they may bear sons and daughters; multiply there, and do not decrease (Jer. 29:6).

Every passage in the Bible affirms the value of children and of having many children. There are no Scriptures that encourage families to desire few children. Jesus expressed the importance and value of children and how we should view them.

> But Jesus said, "Let the little children come to me and do not hinder them, for to such belongs the kingdom of heaven" (Matt. 19:14).

Is There a Perfect Homeschooling Family?

The truth is, some families have very personal and private reasons for why they do not have many children. We should not presume to know their thoughts or motives, nor should we look down on them if their family does not look like ours.

No other family can ever be the standard for our family. We must look to God alone and to His Word for guidance on everything that relates to our family. There should be no spirit of competition among homeschoolers, only love and support. There should be no condescension or fault finding in our brothers and sisters in Christ.

We are not to be the Holy Spirit for other families. We have enough going on in our own homes to keep us busy. It is not our job to ensure that other people homeschool "the right way" or meet up to our preconceived ideas of what their family should look like. It's not our jurisdiction to police other people's homes. One of the best things to do, as it relates to impacting other people, is to live well. If you are living a life that pleases God, and you are loving others as He desires, you will likely have people approach you seeking advice and counsel on struggles they face in their family. This gives you a great privilege to pray with them and help to bear their burdens.

No two homeschooling families will (or should) look exactly alike. Walk humbly before God, always willing to learn and grow, but don't become intimidated into needing to fit into someone else's box. God wants you to be you, not some other family at the homeschool co-op. If you don't feel like you fit into a particular subculture, whether in the world, the Church, or the homeschooling community, that's okay. You don't have to. You just need to follow God through the Bible, and trust that the Holy Spirit will lead and guide you into all truth (see John 16:13).

Endnotes

1. For the latest figures, visit the Centers for Disease Control's (CDC) "Vital Statistics Rapid Release" data: https://www.cdc.gov/nchs/ products/vsrr/natality-dashboard.htm.

2. For a list of fertility rates globally, visit: https://www.cia.gov/library/ publications/the-world-factbook/rankorder/2127rank.html.

3. "Barna Survey Examines Changes in Worldview Among Christians over the Past 13 Years," Research Releases in Faith & Christianity, March 9, 2009, www.barna.com/research/barna-survey-examines-changes-in-worldview-among-christians-over-the-past-13-years.

4. "The Scholastic Achievement and Demographic Characteristics of Home School Students in 1998" by Lawrence M. Rudner, Ph.D. A copy of the full report can be found at (https://www.hslda.org/docs/ study/rudner1999/FullText.asp), or see the peer-reviewed online journal Education Policy Analysis Archives at http://epaa.asu.edu/epaa/v7n8/.

CHAPTER 25

How Should I Respond to Opposition?

Parents who make the choice to teach their children at home are swimming upstream. They are not only making the more costly and laborious decision to take responsibility for teaching their children themselves, but they are also making the most unpopular choice as well.

Homeschoolers in the United States (and even more so around the world) are in the minority when it comes to schooling preference. In almost all states, even costly private schools host more students than home educators.

People of every generation take the broad and popular road. Those who take a narrow path are often regarded as radicals or renegades from society. While they are sometimes lauded long after their death, people like John Wycliffe, William Tyndale, Martin Luther, John Bunyan, and others were despised, persecuted, and even sometimes killed for being social reformers because they did not just fit in and go along with popular opinion.

The Old Days

Trailblazers and pioneers take a lot of heat because they are the ones out front. A scout on a trail is going to be the first one to be attacked if there is a hostile enemy in the path. Those who follow later usually have a much easier time once the trees have been cleared, a road has been paved, and there is an accurate map to follow.

We are grateful for the sacrifices made by the homeschooling families of the 1970s, '80s, and '90s. They have made it so much easier for everyone who has come along since.

Today

Homeschooling has grown by leaps and bounds since its resurgence in 1983. We've gone from a few hundred Christian families in the 1970s to over 2.5 million home educating students in the U.S. in 2015.[1] Almost everyone today knows someone who is currently homeschooling or has been home educated.

This does not mean, however, that everyone appreciates or approves of the practice. While it is far more socially acceptable, and in some circles perhaps it is even a bit of a fad to homeschool, it is still usually met with skepticism and resistance by most people. Even most churches have been hesitant to endorse the practice, and some pressure homeschoolers to put their children into government schools to be "salt and light."

Conviction or Preference?

The reason the reformers I mentioned earlier, and most of the homeschooling pioneers, were not deterred, even in the face of great opposition, was the fact that they were driven by conviction and not mere preference. A conviction is rooted in knowledge. It is based on a certainty that one has made the right choice and is doing what is best.

The reason I wrote my book *Education: Does God Have an Opinion?* was to help Christian parents understand the biblical basis for taking ownership of the discipleship of their own children. When someone understands what God has said in His Word on a matter, it changes everything. Most evangelical Christians have never taken the time to study what the Bible teaches on education. Some home-educating parents are driven, for the most part, by pragmatism, rather than biblical conviction. They are either reacting against a bad experience in the government school system or they are merely picking what looks the best to them on the educational smorgasbord.

If you are homeschooling merely as an academic preference, it is very likely that you will be discouraged and dissuaded once opposition or difficulty comes along. I strongly encourage you to pick up a copy of my other book and prayerfully consider the arguments made in that book concerning a biblical philosophy of education. It has been a definite game-changer for the clear majority of its readers. I've heard numerous reports from parents who say that, after reading it, it led them to certainty and resolve in their decision to home educate in a way nothing else had.

Dealing with the Naysayers

In the Book of Nehemiah, God called His people to an important task: rebuilding the walls of Jerusalem after the exile. In chapter 4, two characters emerge with an intent to derail God's purposes and discourage the workers. Sanballat and Tobiah are reflective of the opposition that will emerge any time people are engaged in profitable activity that builds up God's Kingdom. They mocked and ridiculed (vs. 2–3) and even got angry at God's people (vs. 1 and 7). They schemed together to create confusion, fear, and discord (vs. 8).

How did Nehemiah stand up against these enemies of God's work? First of all, he cried out to God for justice (vs. 4–5). Secondly, he continued doing the work (vs. 6). Third, he prayed and set up a guard for protection (vs. 9). Fourth, he had the people surround themselves with others who were equally committed to the task, so they could work together (vs. 13). He encouraged the laborers by saying, "Do not be afraid of them. Remember the Lord, who is great and awesome, and fight for your brothers, your sons, your daughters, your wives, and your homes" (vs. 14).

This is a great reminder for us as Christian parents that we need to be willing to fight against anything that seeks to wage war for the souls of our children. Don't allow anyone or anything to deter you from your relentless pursuit of family unity and godly living.

In chapter 6, when they saw that their intimidation tactics didn't work, they requested a special meeting with Nehemiah, with the intent to hurt him (vs. 2). But Nehemiah did not give them the time of day. He provides a great model for us about not allowing ourselves to become distracted from the work of the Lord.

"I am doing a great work and I cannot come down. Why should the work stop while I leave it and come down to you?" (vs. 3). They entreated him four times, but he continued to stay focused on the task at hand. In verse 9, Nehemiah recognized his enemies could not sabotage the work of the Lord, but he could if he gave into their pressure. "For they all wanted to frighten us, thinking, 'Their hands will drop from the work, and it will not be done.' But now, O God, strengthen my hands."

Stay the Course

I often say, "Never apologize for being a good parent!" God has given your children to you, not to anyone else. He has entrusted them into your care because He believes that you are the one who is best equipped to be able to make the right decisions for them. Never give into the pressure of trying to conform to someone else's expectations of what you should be doing. Of course, we should be willing to listen and consider the advice and admonitions of wise and godly counselors. But our final authority needs to be the Word of God. What does the Bible teach us about God's will regarding how we should raise our children?

We need to guard our hearts against bitterness or resentment toward those who oppose us. We need to be kind and respectful to them. Very often, these same people will change their opinions later, once they see that their opinions were based largely on ignorance and conjecture rather than fact and biblical support.

I remember my grandmother in 1982 telling us when we visited her church: "Whatever you do, don't tell anyone you don't go to school!" She was embarrassed and ashamed of the fact that we didn't attend a "regular school" like "normal children." I had to chuckle to myself, though, in 2012 when she boldly told someone, speaking of my children: "My great-grandchildren here are homeschooled! They are so smart, and so polite and so helpful. I think everyone should homeschool their children!"

Thirty years of observation of good fruit in the lives of her grandchildren and great-grandchildren changed her mind on the issue. Luke 7:35 (NIV) reveals, "(W)isdom is proved right by all her children." Your task is not to convert the naysayers to your point of view. Your task is to be faithful to lovingly live out the life to which God has called you. Let Him take care of your detractors. Just remember that you are not alone. Do like Nehemiah and find other likeminded believers who are committed to the same task you are. Encourage one another and don't give up. "And let us not grow weary of doing good, for in due season we will reap, if we do not give up" (Gal. 6:9).

Homeschooling Opens Doors to Share the Gospel

I can't tell you how many conversations have opened because of my experience being home educated (or the fact that we teach our own children at home). People are often curious and have a lot of questions. Some of their questions may feel antagonistic or aggressive at first, but often people are afraid of what they don't know. Most people have reservations and concerns about home education, and we have a great opportunity to introduce them to a positive perspective on the topic.

When people ask us why we teach our children, it gives a great open door to sharing our faith in the Lord Jesus Christ. We can tell them about our desire to pass our faith and values on to our children. This can lead to talking with them about their beliefs, and sharing the gospel with them. We should be "prepared to make a defense to anyone who asks you for a reason for the hope that is in you; yet do it with gentleness and respect" (1 Pet. 3:15). Rather than being defensive and taking offense by people's aggressive questioning, we should see it as an opportunity to represent Christ.

What If My Spouse Doesn't Want Me to Homeschool?

One of the hardest scenarios is when a spouse (especially a husband) doesn't want to homeschool, and you do. In my book, *Full-Time Parenting: A Guide to Family-Based Discipleship*, I outline the biblical principles for a wife in making a "godly appeal" to her husband. There is a proper way to express a desire or concern that does not need to include nagging or quarreling. I have known some women who have decided to "put their husbands in their place" and tell him that they plan to homeschool no matter what he thinks. The problem with this approach is that it is almost impossible to effectively raise your children when you are experiencing marital conflict. When a house is divided against itself, it cannot stand (Matt. 12:25).

Many husbands (sadly) will reluctantly "allow" their wives to homeschool, even if they feel that it is a bad idea. Some put a lot of pressure on their wives by constantly saying they fear they will ruin the children. As I explain in the chapter for dads, it is really, chiefly, the father that God holds responsible for the upbringing of the children, not primarily the wife. The wife is to help the husband as he seeks to lead the family in the ways of the Lord, not the other way around.

When a husband flatly refuses to allow the wife to homeschool, there is little she can do (without creating a civil war in the home). She should appeal and clearly articulate her desires, but as much as I hate to say it, I don't see that defying her husband is a good solution. Getting divorced over homeschooling is not going to be good for the children. Pray that God will change your spouse's heart. Resources like the book and video *Indoctrination: Public Schools and the Decline of Christianity*, and my book *Education: Does God Have an Opinion?* are great resources for helping to change worldly thinking on this topic. Please go through these books and videos together with your spouse, and talk and pray about it together. You may want to even suggest a one-year trial to give your husband or wife the ability to see how it might work for your family. One year will certainly not ruin your child's life, even if things go as badly as your spouse fears.

Finding objective research and data on homeschooling success from organizations like HSLDA.org and NHERI.org, is often helpful in convincing skeptics of the validity of homeschooling.

What If My Child Is Resistant to Homeschooling?

It is common, especially for students who have been recently removed from government schools, to miss their friends and desire to rejoin the social atmosphere of the school. This is when it is important to remember that God gives children (and teens) to parents. It is the responsibility of the parent, before God, to make the decisions that they believe are best for the child. Children do not know what is best for them. Children would eat chocolate cake for breakfast every day if they were allowed. In the end, the parent needs to inform the child of the decision of the parents, and communicate lovingly but firmly that the decision is final and not up to debate.

Parents should endeavor to make the learning process at home as enjoyable as possible, but at the end of the day, we all need to learn to accept and embrace things that we don't always enjoy. In any job, there will be things that we do not personally like doing, but we don't give up just because it isn't "fun." Teaching your children to do their best, even if they do not entirely enjoy the process of learning at home, is what is best for them. Be the parent. It's more important that you do the right thing than it is for you to always be "liked" by your child.

In the end, we all answer to one supreme judge: God Himself. He is the one we should seek to please.

> And do not fear those who kill the body but cannot kill the soul. Rather fear him who can destroy both soul and body in hell (Matt. 10:28).

Endnotes
1. NHERI.org.

A BIBLICAL DEFENSE FOR

Homeschooling

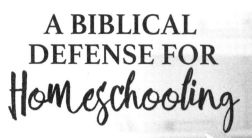

Education:

A BIBLICAL APOLOGETIC FOR CHRISTIAN EDUCATION & HOMESCHOOLING

Does God have an opinion?

Israel Wayne

IF GOD HAS A DEFINITE OPINION ABOUT THE ISSUE OF EDUCATION, WOULDN'T YOU DESIRE TO FIND OUT WHAT IT IS AND HOW BEST TO IMPLEMENT HIS WISDOM?